Denmark On A Budget

Unveiling Eco-Friendly Travels to Earth's Happiest Nation (Sustainable travel trend)

Moon Diamond

Table Of Contents

PART 1: Planning Your Trip

Chapter 1

Welcome to Denmark, Land of Hygge and Fairy Tales!

Picture this: crisp air kissed by the Baltic Sea, sunlight dappling through ancient beech forests, cobbled streets whispering stories of Vikings and mermaids. This, my friend, is Denmark, a tapestry woven from fairy tales and modern marvels, where charming villages nuzzle alongside sleek skyscrapers, and every nook promises a cozy corner to curl up with a good book (or a steaming cup of something warm, because let's be honest, Denmark and hygge go hand in hand).

But before you hop on a Viking longship and set sail (metaphorically speaking, of course, unless you're

feeling particularly adventurous!), let's delve into the nitty-gritty of planning your Danish adventure.
 This guidebook is your trusty map, your friendly barista pouring you a shot of wanderlust, your whispered secret to unlocking the magic of this Scandinavian gem.

About this Guidebook

Think of this as your pocket-sized Gandalf, leading you through rolling hills and storybook towns. We'll cover everything from navigating the quirky charm of Copenhagen to scaling windswept dunes on the Jutland Peninsula, from savoring melt-in-your-mouth pastries to kayaking through emerald fjords. We'll be your confidante, your translator (those Danish vowels can be tricky!), and your shoulder to cry on when you realize you've fallen head over heels for this enchanting land (spoiler alert: it's highly likely).

What to Know Before You Go

Hygge (pronounced hoo-guh):
This isn't just a word, it's a way of life. Think cozy candlelight, crackling fireplaces, and mugs overflowing with hot cocoa. Embrace the hygge, and Denmark will embrace you right back.

Bikes, bikes, bikes:
 Copenhagen is a two-wheeled wonderland. Ditch the taxis and hop on a trusty steed (they're everywhere!), feeling the wind in your hair as you zip past colorful houses and elegant palaces.

Danish Delights:
 New Nordic cuisine is all the rage, and for good reason. Think fresh, seasonal ingredients, innovative twists on classics, and enough smørrebrød (open-faced sandwiches piled high with goodness) to keep you fueled for a lifetime of exploring.

Embrace the outdoors:
 Denmark is a nature lover's paradise. Hike through ancient forests, kayak through glassy fjords, or simply unwind on sun-drenched beaches. The fresh air and stunning scenery are the perfect antidote to any city blues.

Tips for Planning Your Trip

Season Savvy:
Spring paints the country in vibrant greens and pinks, summer brings long, sun-drenched days, autumn explodes in fiery colors, and winter transforms Denmark into a cozy wonderland. Choose your adventure!

Festival Fun:
From Viking reenactments to vibrant music festivals, Denmark's calendar is bursting with events. Do your research and plan your trip around something that sparks your joy.

Getting Around:
 Trains, buses, and ferries whisk you effortlessly across the country. And don't forget the magic of the Öresund Bridge, connecting Denmark to Sweden by train in a blink.

Danish Crowns:

Euros will get you by in a pinch, but having some Danish kroner on hand shows respect and opens doors (literally, sometimes!).

So, are you ready to dive into the Danish dream? Buckle up, adventurer, because this journey promises to be epic. In our next chapter, we'll unlock the secrets of Copenhagen, the vibrant heart of this captivating country. Get your walking shoes ready, we've got cobbled streets and charming canals to conquer!

Chapter 2

Getting There, Getting Around, and Not Getting Lost (Hopefully...)

Alright, your heart's set on Denmark, smørrebrød dreams dancing in your head. But before you start packing your Viking helmet and inflatable kayak (trust me, I've contemplated it too), let's tackle the logistics. Getting to and around Denmark is a breeze, once you know the tricks. Think of this chapter as your personal GPS, minus the robotic lady telling you to "**recalculate**" when you inevitably take a wrong turn (been there, done that, ended up in a field of sheep).

Transportation Options

Flying:
Copenhagen Airport, also known as Kastrup, is your main gateway. It's sleek, efficient, and has enough cinnamon rolls in the arrivals hall to make you weep tears of joy. Plenty of airlines jet there from all corners of the globe, so finding a flight is like picking out your favorite flavor of gummy bear (except without the sugar crash, hopefully).

By Sea:
Ah, the ferry! Think Viking longships without the pillaging (unless you really want to, I won't judge). Boats connect Denmark to neighboring countries like Germany, Sweden, and Norway, offering a scenic, seafaring alternative. Imagine salty air whipping your

hair, seagulls squawking overhead, and a plate of pickled herring magically appearing in your hand (okay, maybe not the last part, but a guy can dream).

Train:
 For the eco-conscious adventurer, the train is a dream. The Danish rail network is like a well-oiled Viking chariot, whisking you from city to city in comfort and style. Picture plush seats, panoramic windows showcasing rolling fields and charming villages, and a smørrebrød buffet in the dining car (not guaranteed, but hey, a traveler can dream).

Getting Around

Copenhagen:
 This city is all about two wheels and two feet. Grab a bike (they're everywhere!), and join the throngs of happy cyclists pedaling through cobbled streets and leafy parks. Or, lace up your walking shoes and get lost in the charming maze of canals, colorful houses, and hidden courtyards. Trust me, your calves will thank you later (maybe not at first, but later, definitely).

Beyond Copenhagen:
 Trains and buses will whisk you to far-flung corners of Denmark. Think Jutland's windswept dunes, fairytale islands like Bornholm, and historic towns like Aarhus with its Viking museum (helmet not required, but encouraged). Just remember to validate your ticket on the train (those little yellow machines are your friends, not your foes).

Navigating

Maps.me is your savior, offline and free. Download it before you go, and thank me later when you're deep in the Danish countryside with no internet and a sheep staring at you expectantly. Signs are usually in English too, but just in case, brush up on a few Danish phrases like "tak" (thank you) and "undskyld" (sorry, especially useful if you accidentally run over someone's bicycle, which, hopefully, you won't).

Pro Tip:
 Learn to pronounce "**smørrebrød**" like a pro. It's "**smoor-bruh-brod**," not "**smur-fur-bread**." Trust

me, you'll earn major brownie points (or maybe smørrebrød points?) with the locals.

Remember, getting lost is half the fun. So wander, explore, and embrace the detours. You might just stumble upon a hidden gem, a secret bakery with pastries that will make your eyes water (in a good way), or a cozy pub with Vikings singing sea shanties (okay, maybe not, but wouldn't that be epic?).

Getting Your Danish Wheels Spinning: From Rolling Bikes to Cozy Trains

Fellow adventurer, we've touched down in Denmark, bellies rumbling for smørrebrød and hearts aflutter with excitement. But how do we navigate this charming land? Fear not, intrepid explorer, for this chapter is your transportation compass, guiding you through the maze of bikes, trains, and maybe even a Viking chariot (okay, maybe not, but wouldn't that be epic?).

Public Transport

Denmark's public transport system is like a well-oiled Viking longship, whisking you around with efficiency and, dare I say, a touch of hygge. Trains, buses, and metro lines crisscross the country, connecting cities, towns, and even sleepy hamlets with charming names you'll struggle to pronounce (but hey, that's half the fun, right?).

Copenhagen:
Buckle up, city slicker, because Copenhagen's public transport is a dream. The metro is sleek and speedy, gliding through the city like a silver snake. Trains connect you to the suburbs and beyond, while buses weave through charming streets, offering front-row seats to the Danish way of life. And don't forget the harbor boats, bobbing gently on the canals, offering a watery perspective on the city's beauty.

Beyond Copenhagen:
Don't let the city lights steal your thunder. Trains whisk you to Aarhus, Denmark's second city, with its vibrant student scene and Viking museum (helmet not required, but encouraged). Buses meander through rolling hills and charming villages, while ferries hop

between islands like Bornholm, a fairytale escape
with dramatic cliffs and sandy beaches.

Top Tip:
 Download the Rejseplanen app, your Danish transport
BFF. It spits out timetables, maps, and even tells you
which platform to stand on (no more sprinting down
corridors with your suitcase like a runaway suitcase
troll).

Taxis and Ridesharing

Sometimes, you just need a chariot (okay, a taxi) to
whisk you away in style. Taxis are readily available in
larger cities, though be prepared for a dent in your
kroner stash. Ridesharing apps like Uber are also
gaining traction, offering a convenient alternative
(just remember to check your internet connection
before venturing out to rural areas, where your
phone might become a glorified paperweight).

Renting a Car

For the free spirits and open-road enthusiasts, renting a car unlocks a treasure trove of adventures. Imagine cruising down coastal highways with the Baltic Sea sparkling on one side and windswept dunes on the other. Just remember, Danes drive on the right side of the road (unlike those quirky Brits), and parking in Copenhagen can be a Tetris-level challenge.

Biking and Walking

Embrace your inner Viking (minus the pillaging, of course) and hop on a bike! Denmark is a cyclist's paradise, with dedicated lanes, friendly drivers, and enough fresh air to clear your lungs and your head. Copenhagen is especially bike-friendly, with its network of paths and a culture that practically worships two wheels. And for the walkers among us, lace up your shoes and prepare to be enchanted. Winding cobbled streets, hidden courtyards, and charming canals await, each step a postcard comes to life.

Top Tip:

Invest in a good rain jacket. Danish weather can be as unpredictable as a Viking berserker, so be prepared for a sprinkle (or a downpour) every now and then.

Remember, the best way to get around Denmark is the way that sparks your joy. So, whether you're a two-wheeled warrior, a train-hopping nomad, or a taxi-loving adventurer, embrace the journey and let Denmark weave its magic around you.

Chapter 3

Finding Your Danish Hygge Haven

From Boutique Bunkies to Castle Dreams

Alright, we've conquered the transportation beast, and your stomach's probably doing the Viking war cry for smørrebrød. But before we dive into that deliciousness, let's find you a cozy Danish nest to curl up in after a day of exploring. Choosing your accommodation is like picking your perfect fairytale setting: do you want a chic castle overlooking the sea, a quirky guesthouse with a talking raven (okay, maybe not, but wouldn't that be epic?), or a vibrant hostel buzzing with fellow adventurers? Fear not, for this chapter is your personal Danish digs decoder, helping you find the perfect place to rest your weary head and dream of Viking conquests (or maybe just a really good pastry).

Choosing Your Hygge Hub

First things first, where does your Danish heart yearn to be? Copenhagen's vibrant streets beckon with trendy lofts and canal-side havens. Jutland's windswept dunes whisper of cozy cottages and stargazing getaways. Or maybe you crave the island serenity of Bornholm, where charming guest houses with thatched roofs promise whispered secrets of the Baltic Sea.

Budget Buccaneers

Hostels are your best friends, offering bunks for budget-minded explorers. Think clean, comfortable dorms, social common areas where you can swap stories with fellow adventurers, and maybe even a friendly ghost or two (okay, maybe not, but the Danes love a good ghost story). Copenhagen's Danhostel Copenhagen City is a backpacker's paradise, while Aarhus Hostel boasts a cool industrial vibe and a rooftop terrace that's perfect for watching the sunset paint the city gold.

Boutique Bunkies

For those seeking a touch of hipster hygge, Copenhagen's boutique hotels are a dream come true. Imagine exposed brick walls, vintage furniture with stories to tell, and maybe even a rooftop bar with views that will make you weak in the knees (and not just from the schnapps, I promise). Hotel SP34 is a design lover's haven, while Manoy Copenhagen offers Scandi chic with a side of harbor views.

Castle Dreams

Let's be honest, who doesn't secretly dream of sleeping in a real-life castle? Denmark has you covered, from the majestic Kronborg Castle, where Shakespeare's Hamlet once roamed the ramparts, to the fairytale-like Dragsholm Slot, with its moat, towers, and whispers of medieval feasts. Just remember, these beauties come with a hefty price tag, so start saving your kroner (or maybe invent a time machine and marry a prince, whatever works!).

Top Tip:
 Book early, especially during peak season! Danes love their hygge as much as you do, and those cozy nooks fill up fast.

Remember, your accommodation is more than just a place to sleep, it's an experience. So choose wisely, adventurer, and let your Danish digs be the launching pad for adventures extraordinaire.

Home Away from Hygge

Unlocking the Doors to Danish Dwelling Delights

Alright, we've found our Viking feet, figured out where to lay our weary heads, and now our stomachs are doing the war cry for smørrebrød (seriously, can we talk about those open-faced beauties?). But before we indulge in all that deliciousness, let's delve into the realm of Danish dwellings, where your temporary home won't just be a place to crash, but a launchpad for epic adventures. Think charming cottages with thatched roofs, sleek apartments overlooking glittering canals, or maybe even a cozy tent under a sky dusted with a million stars. Buckle up, because this chapter is your key to unlocking the perfect Danish digs, no matter your budget or inner Viking spirit.

Vacation Rentals

Craving a slice of Danish life? Vacation rentals are your jam. Imagine a quaint cottage nestled amidst rolling hills, a modern apartment buzzing with urban energy, or a beachfront villa with waves whispering secrets to your doorstep. Airbnb is your best friend here, offering apartments with quirky charm, houses with enough space for the whole Viking clan, and maybe even a treehouse or two (because who wouldn't want to sleep in a freaking treehouse?).

Top Tip:
 Be a savvy smørrebrød-budgeting beast and book early, especially during peak season. Those charming Danish nooks get snatched up faster than a pastry at a free smørrebrød buffet (yes, those exist, and yes, they're magical).

Homestays and Apartments

Want to experience hygge on a deeper level? Homestays are where it's at. Imagine living with a Danish family, chatting over steaming cups of kaffe (that's coffee, but way cooler), learning their secret smørrebrød recipes (don't worry, I won't tell if you lick the plate), and maybe even joining them for a game of Viking chess (don't ask me the rules, I'm still figuring them out). Websites like HomestayDenmark connect you with welcoming families, while apartments offer independent living with a touch of local charm.

Camping and Glamping

For the wild Viking at heart, Denmark's embrace stretches to the great outdoors. Imagine pitching your tent under a canopy of stars, listening to the waves crash against the shore, and waking up to a symphony of birdsong. Campsites dot the country, offering everything from basic pitches to glamping tents fit for a modern-day warrior queen (complete with plush beds and maybe even a hot tub, because even Vikings deserve a little pampering).

Top Tip:

Embrace the Danish love for nature! Pack your hiking boots, swimsuits, and maybe even a kayak. You'll never regret exploring the hidden gems Denmark has tucked away in its meadows, forests, and fjords.

Remember, your Danish dwelling is more than just a roof over your head, it's a portal to unforgettable experiences. So choose wisely, adventurer, and let your home away from home be the springboard for adventures that will have you weaving your own Danish fairy tales long after you've returned home.

Chapter 4

Packing Like a Viking

Conquering the Danish Wardrobe

Alright, adventurer, we've found our Danish digs, our stomachs are doing Viking war cries for smørrebrød, and our hearts are pounding like war drums with excitement. But before we charge headfirst into a smorgasbord of adventures, let's talk about essentials – the stuff that'll keep you comfy, confident, and ready to conquer Denmark, one cobbled street and windswept dune at a time. Think of this chapter as your personal packing guru, whispering secrets of layers, hygge-approved knits, and maybe even a waterproof Viking helmet (okay, maybe not, but wouldn't that be epic?).

Clothing and Footwear

Denmark's weather is like a mischievous elf, changing moods faster than a Viking warrior in battle. So, layers are your best friend. Pack breathable tees for sunny days, cozy sweaters for chilly evenings, and a waterproof jacket that can handle anything a Nordic squall throws your way. Jeans are a trusty standby, but don't forget comfy pants for exploring charming villages and maybe even a flowy dress for those sun-soaked moments by the water (because let's be honest, you'll want to twirl like a fairytale princess at some point).

Shoe-wise, think versatility. Sturdy boots for treks through windswept dunes, comfy sneakers for pounding Copenhagen's cobbled streets, and maybe even sandals for those lazy afternoons by the harbor. And don't forget a good pair of socks – wool if you're feeling extra Viking, regular if you're a more modern-day adventurer.

Top Tip:
 Embrace the Danes' love for hygge! Pack a chunky knit scarf, a cozy beanie, and maybe even a pair of wool socks (because let's face it, there's nothing cozier than curling up with a good book and a steaming cup of kaffe on a chilly Danish evening).

Toiletries and Personal Care

The usual suspects apply here: toothbrush, toothpaste, sunscreen (Danish sun can be surprisingly sneaky!), and maybe even a travel-sized bottle of your favorite shampoo (unless you're feeling adventurous and want to try the local Viking hair tonic – just don't blame me if you end up with braids and a thirst for mead). For the ladies, pack your usual lady-business essentials, and for the gents, well, just remember, deodorant is your friend, especially after a day of conquering Viking obstacle courses (or maybe just climbing a few hills).

Electronics and Accessories

Phone, charger, camera – the holy trinity of modern-day adventuring. Don't forget an adapter, because Danish plugs like to play hide-and-seek with American ones. A portable power bank is your savior in a world obsessed with capturing every smørrebrød masterpiece and fairytale sunset. And for the music lovers, pack your headphones and get ready to blast some Viking anthems as you explore (just be mindful of your fellow adventurers, not everyone wants to hear your rendition of **"Hakuna Matata"** at full volume).

Top Tip:
 Pack a reusable water bottle! Denmark is all about sustainability, and staying hydrated is key for conquering castles and conquering those

post-smørrebrød sugar crashes. Plus, you'll save yourself a fortune on bottled water (which you can then spend on more pastries, obviously).

Remember, adventurer, packing is like an art form. It's about striking the perfect balance between preparedness and wanderlust. So, choose wisely, pack light, and embrace the Danish spirit of hygge and adventure. In our next chapter, Copenhagen awaits, with its colorful canals, quirky museums, and enough Tivoli Gardens magic to make you believe in fairytales again. Buckle up, it's going to be epic!

P.S. And hey, if you really want to channel your inner Viking, pack a tiny plastic horn. You never know when you might need to sound a battle cry for smørrebrød supremacy!

Medications And Prescriptions

Alright, buckle up, friend, because we're taking a deep dive into Denmark! Now, this isn't just some dry guidebook spiel, we're gonna explore this Viking wonderland like two mates over a steaming mug of gløgg, spilled secrets and all.

First things first, let's talk

pharmaceuticals

Denmark's healthcare system is top-notch, but here's the rub: prescriptions aren't exactly handed out like candy on Halloween. If you're on regular meds, pack that stash like it's gold bullion. Don't even think about winging it with a "borrowed" prescription – you'll get the stink eye quicker than you can say "smørrebrød." Trust me, a Danish customs agent giving you the side-eye is colder than a fjord in February.

Speaking of packing, let's get seasonal with it. **Summer in Denmark** is like a flirty teenager – warm enough for sundresses and picnics, but prone to dramatic mood swings. One minute you're basking in sunshine, the next you're dodging hailstones the size of kumquats. Pack layers, my friend, layers like an onion with a PhD in meteorology. Don't forget a raincoat that folds small enough to fit in your pocket, because Danish rain doesn't announce itself with polite thunderclaps – it just shows up like an uninvited guest with a soggy handshake.

Autumn in Denmark is pure cozy magic. Think fireplaces crackling, leaves crunching underfoot, and that special kind of hygge that makes you want to bake a million cinnamon buns and wear fuzzy socks 24/7. Pack sweaters that feel like hugs, boots that can handle crunchy leaves and rogue puddles, and a scarf big enough to double as a blanket when you inevitably doze off in a sunbeam. Don't forget a camera, because the colors explode across the landscape like an Impressionist painting dipped in maple syrup.

Winter in Denmark is a whole different beast. It's like Narnia and Mordor had a snow baby, and that baby decided to throw a rave in Copenhagen. Dress for the Arctic apocalypse, with layers upon layers of thermals, a waterproof coat that could withstand a Viking longship raid, and boots that make you look like you could conquer Everest in your sleep. Pack hand warmers, a hat that wouldn't look out of place on a Yeti, and a sense of humor – you'll need it when you slip on black ice and land in a snowdrift looking like a human snowball. But hey, there's something undeniably exhilarating about walking through a winter wonderland where the only sound is your own crunching footsteps.

Spring in Denmark is like a shy teenager finally coming out of its shell. The sun starts peeking out more often, flowers poke their heads through the thawing earth, and everyone gets a case of the spring fever. Pack lighter layers, something waterproof for those April showers, and a good pair of walking shoes because you'll be drawn outside like a moth to a flame. Pack your camera too, because the Danes have a serious knack for turning even a tiny patch of dirt into a blooming masterpiece.

And remember, no matter what season you choose, pack your sense of adventure and a willingness to embrace the unexpected. Denmark is a land of quirky charm, endless hygge, and enough pastries to make your dentist weep. So go forth, explore, and don't forget to bring back a Viking helmet and a fistful of licorice allsorts as souvenirs. Just promise me you won't try the gammeldansk hakkebøf – trust me, your taste buds will thank you.

Now, if you'll excuse me, I have a date with a steaming mug of gløgg and a plate of smørrebrød piled high with herring.

Chapter 5

Budget Planning

Alright, let's crack open the piggy bank and get real about the Danish kroner – budget time! Now, Denmark ain't exactly known for its bargain-basement prices, but hey, with a little planning and some savvy tips, you can have a Viking-worthy adventure without breaking the bank of Valhalla.

Flights, my friend, are the big kahuna. Prices fluctuate like a longboat in a storm, so be flexible with your dates and keep an eye on those deals. Skyscanner and Google Flights are your budget-savvy sidekicks, constantly whispering sweet nothings of price drops and hidden gems. Don't be afraid to mix and match airlines or consider flying into nearby airports – sometimes saving a few kroner means a detour, but hey, that just adds to the adventure, right?

Accommodation:
Now, this is where things get interesting. Hostels are your budget BFFs, offering bunks for the price of a fancy cocktail. Plus, you'll meet fellow adventurers and swap stories over free breakfast (usually involving rye bread and enough jam to fuel a dragon). If hostels aren't your jam, consider Airbnbs or smaller, locally-owned hotels. They're often cheaper than the big chains and come with the added bonus of local charm and insider tips. Just remember, Copenhagen is pricier than the countryside, so factor that in when choosing your home base.

Food, glorious food:
ah, the smørrebrød, the pastries, the endless cups of coffee! Eating out in Denmark can be a budget buster, but fear not, hunger pangs! Supermarkets are your secret weapon. Stock up on picnic-friendly goodies, grab fresh bread and cheese for DIY smørrebrød (it's easier than you think, promise!), and cook a few meals in your Airbnb. Trust me, nothing beats savoring a picnic in a sun-drenched park or

whipping up a feast with local ingredients. Plus, you'll get to experience the Danish supermarket scene, which is an adventure in itself (think licorice allsorts and pickled herring – not for the faint of heart!).

Activities and tours:
 Now, this is where you gotta decide what floats your Viking ship. Museums can be pricey, but many offer free entry on certain days or have discounted student/senior rates. Don't underestimate the power of free stuff – walking tours, parks, and historical sites are often your best bet for budget-friendly entertainment. Plus, Denmark is made for exploring on foot or by bike, so lace up your shoes and hit the pavement – you'll discover hidden gems and local secrets you wouldn't find on any tour bus.

Here's a little insider tip: Copenhagen Card. It's like a magic passport to free public transport, museum entry, and discounts on tons of activities. If you're planning on doing a lot of sightseeing, it can be a real money-saver. But remember, do the math! Sometimes, paying for individual activities might be cheaper depending on your plans.

And finally, a budgeting life hack: embrace the hygge! Cozy nights in with board games, roasting marshmallows over a bonfire, or simply curling up with a good book can be just as magical (and wallet-friendly) as any fancy outing. Remember, Denmark is all about slowing down and enjoying the simple things.

So, there you have it! With a little planning and some creative thinking, you can conquer Denmark on a budget. Just remember, the best souvenirs are the memories you make, not the kroner you spend. Now go forth, explore, and let the hygge guide you! And hey, if you do go all-out on a fancy Viking feast, well, I won't judge...much. Skål!

Conquering Copenhagen and Beyond

Budget Hacks for the Savvy Traveler

Listen up, budget warriors and penny-pinching pilgrims, because we're about to crack the code on conquering Denmark without breaking the bank! This

ain't your average travel guide, nah, this is a
Viking-sized helping of insider tips and tricks to turn
you into a kroner-saving champion. So grab your
metaphorical mead horn and raise it high, because
Denmark awaits, and your wallet will thank you for it!

Food Glorious Food

Let's be honest, Danish cuisine is epic, but it can also
be epic-ly expensive. Fear not, famished friends,
because there's a smorgasbord of ways to satisfy
your inner foodie without sending your budget on a
one-way trip to Valhalla.

Supermarket Savvy:
 Embrace the inner Dane and hit the local grocery
stores. Picnics in the park are a national pastime, and
with fresh bread, meats, cheeses, and spreads, you
can whip up a smørrebrød feast fit for a king (or
queen!). Plus, you'll get a taste of the Danish culinary
scene without the restaurant markup. Just don't
forget the kaffe – Danes take their coffee seriously,
and a flask of the good stuff can fuel your
adventures for hours.

Market Magic:
Dive into the vibrant atmosphere of Copenhagen's
Torvehallerne Market. Sample local delicacies, hunt
for fresh produce, and maybe even snag a deal on
some artisanal cheeses. It's a feast for the senses
and the wallet, and you might just stumble upon your
new favorite Danish treat.

Lunchtime Loot:
 Many restaurants offer a cheaper " **dagens frokost**"
(lunch of the day) option. It's usually a hearty,
traditional dish that won't leave your stomach
grumbling or your wallet weeping.

DIY Dining:
 Hostels and Airbnbs often come equipped with
kitchens, so unleash your inner chef and whip up a
culinary masterpiece. It's a great way to save money,
bond with fellow travelers, and impress everyone
with your newfound skills (or at least provide
entertainment with your kitchen mishaps).

Accommodation Adventures

Finding a cozy nest without breaking the bank is key to a budget-friendly Danish adventure. So ditch the fancy hotels and set your sights on these snug spots:

Hostels are your budget besties:
 They're social, they're clean, and they're a treasure trove of travel tips from fellow adventurers. Plus, with bunks starting at around 200 kroner, you'll have more cash for exploring and indulging in all things Danish.

Camping under the stars:
Pitch a tent in one of Denmark's many campsites and get back to nature. It's a budget-friendly way to experience the great outdoors and witness some truly epic sunrises (or maybe even the elusive Northern Lights!). Just be sure to pack warm layers – Danish nights can get crisp, even in summer.

Couchsurfing for the courageous:
 If you're feeling adventurous, why not couchsurf? It's a free way to stay with locals, get insider tips, and experience Danish culture firsthand. Just be

sure to read reviews carefully and choose your hosts wisely.

Tipping Tales

Tipping in Denmark is a bit of a mystery, shrouded in the mist of cultural nuances. But fear not, intrepid traveler, I'm here to demystify the dos and don'ts:

Restaurants:
Generally, tipping isn't expected in Denmark. Service charges are usually included in the bill, so there's no need to feel obligated to leave extra. However, if you have exceptional service and want to show your appreciation, a small round up to the nearest 10 kroner is always welcome.

Taxis:
Again, tipping isn't mandatory, but rounding up to the nearest 10 kroner is a nice gesture.

Hotels:

Housekeeping staff will appreciate a small tip (around 20-30 kroner per night) if you feel their service deserves it.

Remember:
a smile and a genuine "**tak**" (thank you) go a long way in Denmark. So ditch the tipping anxieties and focus on enjoying the Danish charm and hospitality!

With these budget-savvy tips and tricks, you're well on your way to conquering Denmark without breaking the bank. So pack your sense of adventure, your appetite for smørrebrød, and your thirst for hygge, and get ready for an unforgettable Danish escapade! Skål!

PART 2: Exploring Your Destination

Chapter 6

Buckle Up, Buttercup

Diving into Denmark's Must-See Sights!

Alright, we're about to dive deep into the heart of Denmark, where Viking whispers mingle with modern marvels and history hangs heavy in the air. Get ready to fill your camera roll and your memory bank with sights that'll make your friends back home weep with envy. But hold on, before we charge into this smorgasbord of attractions, let's lay out the must-sees, the crème de la crème, the Viking helmets on the top shelf, shall we?

Copenhagen Calling

First stop, the crown jewel, the mermaid herself –
Copenhagen! No trip to Denmark is complete without
gawking at the Little Mermaid statue. Sure, she's
tiny, but hey, even mermaids gotta start somewhere,
right? Plus, the waterfront setting is pure hygge
magic, especially with a warm cinnamon bun in hand.

Speaking of hygge, Rosenborg Castle is like stepping
into a royal fairytale. This Renaissance stunner is
packed with glittering treasures, from crown jewels
that could blind a dragon to tapestries whispering
stories of long-dead kings. Imagine waltzing through
grand halls and peeking into the Crown Room, where
diamonds the size of your thumb glint under the
chandeliers. Pure regal magic, my friend.

For a taste of Viking grit, dive into the National
Museum. Think fearsome axes, intricate rune stones,
and enough Viking bling to make Kanye West jealous.
You'll learn about their seafaring ways, their battles
(spoiler alert: they were fierce!), and how they

basically invented the word **"berserker."** Prepare to be humbled by these legendary badasses.

Beyond the Big City

Copenhagen is just the tip of the iceberg, friend. Let's venture into the Danish countryside, where rolling hills meet windswept coastlines and charming villages ooze with history.

Kronborg Castle in Elsinore is where Shakespeare's Hamlet went all melancholy and skull-clutching. This imposing fortress perched on the sea like a brooding giant will make you feel like you've stepped straight into the play. Just don't expect any actual ghosts – unless you count the ones conjured by your overactive imagination, that is.

Speaking of history, Jelling Mounds in Jutland are like Denmark's answer to Stonehenge, only cooler because of Vikings. These ancient burial mounds, crowned with rune stones that whisper tales of Viking kings and queens, are like stepping back in time. Imagine the feasts, the battles, the epic sagas that unfolded here – it'll give you goosebumps guaranteed.

And for a dose of natural beauty that'll knock your socks off, head to Møns Klint, Denmark's answer to the White Cliffs of Dover. These chalk cliffs rise dramatically from the Baltic Sea, offering breathtaking views and a chance to commune with the wild, windswept spirit of Denmark. Just be careful not to get swept away by the wind – those Vikings were onto something with their helmets, you know?

Remember, this is just a taste of the smorgasbord that is Denmark's must-see sights.
 Every corner of this country is bursting with history, culture, and natural beauty. So grab your walking shoes, your camera, and your thirst for adventure, and get ready to explore! Just promise me you won't try to steal any Viking bling – those guys were serious about their treasure, and I wouldn't want you to end up swimming with the fishes (unless, of course, that's part of your grand adventure, in which case, more power to you!).

Now go forth, explore, and let Denmark weave its magic on you. Skål!

Denmark: Beyond the Smørrebrød - Museums, Nature, and Hidden Gems

Alright, culture vultures and nature lovers, gather 'round! We're taking a deep dive into Denmark's treasures beyond the smørrebrød and Carlsberg (though don't worry, there'll be plenty of that too!). Get ready to fill your eyes with art, your lungs with fresh air, and your soul with the quiet magic of Danish landscapes.

Museum Mania

Denmark's museums are like treasure chests overflowing with history, art, and enough Viking bling to make Kanye West jealous. Here are a few must-sees:

Ny Carlsberg Glyptotek:
Think ancient Greek statues, Egyptian mummies, and Impressionist masterpieces all under one roof. It's like a time-traveling art buffet, and you're invited to feast!

Louisiana Museum of Modern Art:
Perched on the coast, this museum is as much about the setting as the art. Think sleek, modern buildings surrounded by sculpture gardens and panoramic sea views. It's the perfect place to get your fill of contemporary art and fresh air.

ARoS Aarhus Art Museum:
This rainbow-colored behemoth isn't shy about grabbing attention. Inside, you'll find thought-provoking contemporary art, panoramic city views from the rainbow rooftop, and maybe even a giant inflatable boy floating in the sky (don't ask, just go with it).

Nature's Playground

Denmark's not all museums and castles, folks. It's got a wild side too, with dramatic coastlines, rolling hills, and enough forest to make a squirrel blush. Here's a taste:

Wadden Sea National Park:
 Take a boat trip through this UNESCO World Heritage Site and spot seals basking on sandbars, migrating birds painting the sky black, and maybe even a curious porpoise peeking at you from the deep. It's nature's symphony, and you're the conductor.

Møns Klint:
These chalk cliffs rising majestically from the Baltic Sea are like Denmark's answer to the White Cliffs of Dover, only with more wind and fewer tourists (for now). Hike to the top for breathtaking views and a healthy dose of sea spray. Just don't try to reenact Hamlet's cliff-jumping scene – that's best left to the professionals (or the foolhardy, depending on your perspective).

Rebild National Park:

This sprawling forest is Denmark's answer to a fairytale. Think ancient trees whispering secrets, hidden lakes reflecting the sky, and enough hiking trails to make your Fitbit weep with joy. It's the perfect place to reconnect with nature and maybe even stumble upon a gnome or two (okay, maybe not, but a girl can dream!).

Parks and Garden Paradise

For those who prefer their nature manicured (no judgment!), Denmark has some stunning parks and gardens to explore. Here are a couple of standouts:

Kongens Have (King's Garden):
This royal retreat in Copenhagen is like a green oasis in the city. Stroll through formal gardens, rent a rowboat on the lake, and pretend you're a Danish noble enjoying a leisurely afternoon. Just don't wear your crown – unless you want to attract some strange looks.

Tivoli Gardens:

This amusement park is like a fairytale come to life. Think twinkling lights, candy-colored rides, and enough gardens to make a botanist weep with joy. It's the perfect place to unleash your inner child and scream your lungs out on a roller coaster (just don't wake the Queen, who lives nearby).

Off the Beaten Path

Now, for the adventurous souls who like to stray from the tourist trail, here are a few hidden gems:

Dragsholm Slot:
This medieval castle turned luxury hotel is like stepping back in time. Think moat, drawbridge, and enough ghosts to keep you up all night (or maybe that's just the pre-bed Carlsberg talking).

Experimentarium:
This science center in Hellerup is like a playground for grown-ups (and curious kids, of course). Think mind-bending optical illusions, interactive exhibits, and enough scientific fun to make even the most jaded cynic crack a smile.

Alright, alright, I can't leave you hanging with those tantalising hidden gems! Here's the rest of the off-the-beaten-path goodness:

Møns Klint GeoCenter:
Dive into the geological history of Møns Klint at this fascinating visitor center. Learn about fossils, rock formations, and the ongoing battle between land and sea. It's the perfect pit stop before tackling those awe-inspiring cliffs.

Den Blå Planet (The Blue Planet):
Dive into the underwater world at this stunning aquarium in Copenhagen. From playful penguins to majestic sharks, witness the incredible diversity of marine life without getting your shoes wet. Just maybe skip the fried fish after seeing your new fishy friends...

Ribe Viking Center:
 Travel back in time to the Viking era at this interactive museum in Ribe. Learn about their weapons, their ships, and their surprisingly good hygiene (turns out Vikings loved saunas!). You might even get to try your hand at ax-throwing – just don't

blame me if you miss the target (and the audience gasps).

And there you have it, folks! Denmark's hidden gems, ready to be unearthed by adventurous souls like yourselves. Remember, the best experiences are often found off the beaten path, where the crowds thin and the magic thickens. So grab your hiking boots, your sense of wonder, and your willingness to get a little lost (the best kind of lost, of course!). Denmark awaits, with smørrebrød, Vikings, and hidden adventures just waiting to be discovered. Skål!

P.S. Don't forget to pack your bathing suit, just in case you stumble upon a secret Viking hot spring. Those guys knew how to relax in style!

Chapter 7

Beyond the City Walls: Unforgettable Day Trips in Denmark

Alright, explorers, we've conquered the city sights and soaked up the urban hygge. Now, it's time to spread our wings and venture beyond the city limits, where charming villages, dramatic landscapes, and Viking whispers dance on the wind. Buckle up, because we're about to embark on a whirlwind tour of Denmark's best day trips!

Island Hopping Adventure

Denmark's a smorgasbord of islands, each with its own unique flavor. So grab your ferry ticket and let's set sail!

Bornholm:

This sun-drenched island in the Baltic is like a Danish Bali, with sandy beaches, rocky cliffs, and enough smoked herring to make your taste buds sing. Hike through the stunning Almindingen forest, visit the ancient Hammershus fortress, or simply soak up the sun on Dueodde Beach. It's island bliss, Danish-style!

Møn:
Think chalk cliffs rising majestically from the sea, charming villages with thatched roofs, and enough wind to blow your hair back (literally). Hike the cliff trails, explore the medieval town of Stege, or visit the GeoCenter to learn about the island's fascinating geological history. Just don't try to recreate Hamlet's cliff-jumping scene – let's leave that to the professionals (or the very foolish).

Samsø:
This organic island in the Kattegat Sea is like a haven for nature lovers. Cycle through fields of wildflowers, visit the charming village of Ballen with its traditional houses, or sample the island's delicious organic produce. It's the perfect place to unplug, unwind, and reconnect with the simple things.

Castle-Hopping Extravaganza

Denmark's got castles galore, each one whispering tales of knights, princesses, and maybe even a few dragons (okay, maybe not dragons, but you never know!).

Kronborg Castle (Elsinore):
This imposing fortress on the Baltic coast is where Shakespeare's Hamlet went all melancholy and skull-clutching. Explore the ramparts, peek into the royal chambers, and maybe even catch a glimpse of the elusive "**sea ghost**." Just remember, no Elsinore adventures are complete without a selfie beneath the famous "**To Be or Not to Be**" archway.

Frederiksborg Castle:
 Picture a Renaissance beauty perched on three islets in a sparkling lake. That's Frederiksborg Castle, a UNESCO World Heritage Site and a testament to Danish royal extravagance. Wander through the opulent halls, marvel at the gardens, and feel like a king (or queen) for a day. Just don't try on any

crowns – unless you want to attract some very curious stares.

Egeskov Castle:
This fairytale-like castle is surrounded by a moat and filled with quirky treasures. Think a room dedicated to hunting trophies (including a narwhal tusk!), a collection of miniature houses, and even a mummy. It's like stepping into a slightly eccentric history book, and you're the curious protagonist!

Nature's Playground

Denmark's not all castles and cobbled streets, folks. It's got a wild side too, with dramatic coastlines, rolling hills, and enough forest to make a squirrel blush. So lace up your boots and get ready for some fresh air!

Wadden Sea National Park:
Take a boat trip through this UNESCO World Heritage Site and spot seals basking on sandbars, migrating birds painting the sky black, and maybe even a curious porpoise peeking at you from the deep. It's nature's symphony, and you're the conductor

(just don't try conducting the seals – they have their own tunes to sing).

Rebild National Park:
 This sprawling forest is Denmark's answer to a fairytale. Think ancient trees whispering secrets, hidden lakes reflecting the sky, and enough hiking trails to make your Fitbit weep with joy. It's the perfect place to reconnect with nature and maybe even stumble upon a gnome or two (okay, maybe not, but a girl can dream!).

Møns Klint:
These chalk cliffs rising majestically from the Baltic Sea are like Denmark's answer to the White Cliffs of Dover, only with more wind and fewer tourists (for now). Hike to the top for breathtaking views and a healthy dose of sea spray. Just don't try to reenact Hamlet's cliff-jumping scene (Picks up where we left off) ...that's best left to the professionals (or the very foolish).

Beyond the Classics

There's more to Denmark than just the typical tourist trail, folks. So let's venture off the beaten path and discover some hidden gems:

Ribe:
This medieval town in Jutland is like stepping back in time. Wander through cobbled streets lined with half-timbered houses, peek into the Ribe Viking Center, and sample the local delicacies (maybe skip the pickled herring on your first try). It's like a living history museum, and you're the fascinated visitor!

Dragsholm Slot:
 This medieval castle turned luxury hotel is like a scene from a gothic novel. Think spooky towers, secret passages, and maybe even the ghost of a jilted bride wandering the halls (okay, maybe that's just the post-dinner gløgg talking). But seriously, it's a unique and atmospheric place to spend a night, if you're brave enough!

Louisiana Museum of Modern Art:
Perched on the coast north of Copenhagen, this museum is as much about the setting as the art.

Think sleek, modern buildings surrounded by sculpture gardens and panoramic sea views. It's the perfect place to get your fill of contemporary art and fresh air, and maybe even catch a glimpse of the sun sinking into the Baltic Sea.

Remember, the best day trips are often the ones that surprise you.
 So don't be afraid to stray from the tourist guide and explore the corners and crannies of Denmark. You might just stumble upon your own hidden gem, a secret village, a majestic viewpoint, or maybe even a friendly Viking ghost (though let's hope they're more interested in sharing a beer than a battle axe!).

Just pack your sense of adventure, your camera, and maybe a few kroner for those tempting roadside Smørrebrød stands. Denmark awaits, with open arms and endless possibilities for unforgettable day trips. Skål!

P.S. Don't forget to pack your swimsuit, just in case you stumble upon a secret Viking hot spring. Those guys knew how to relax in style!

Alright, let's talk about getting your fill of Danish thrills! Whether you're a tour-loving explorer or a free-wheeling road warrior, Denmark's got something for everyone (except maybe couch potatoes – though even they might be tempted by a cozy castle tour!). So grab your sunblock, your sense of direction, and let's dive into the world of excursions, car rentals, and good old-fashioned shoe leather!

Touring the Danish Delights

For those who like their adventures pre-planned and packed with insider info, organized tours are a golden ticket. Imagine skipping the line at Kronborg Castle, hearing Viking tales whispered across the Wadden Sea, or having a local foodie guide you to the best smørrebrød in Copenhagen. Tours come in all flavors, from history-packed walking tours to nature-loving cycling excursions. Just pick your poison (or should I say, your smørrebrød?), sit back, and let someone else handle the logistics.

Hitting the Road in a Rolling Hygge Machine

If you crave the freedom of the open road and the wind in your hair (or helmet, if you're smart), renting a car is a fantastic option. Imagine cruising through rolling countryside, stopping at charming villages on a whim, and blasting Danish pop music with the windows down (just maybe not within earshot of any locals...). Renting a car gives you the flexibility to explore hidden corners, create your own itinerary, and maybe even stumble upon a secret Viking burial mound (though please, let's leave the digging to the professionals!).

Hiking for Hygge Hearts

Denmark's not just cobblestones and castles, folks. It's got a wild side too, with forests whispering secrets, dramatic coastlines begging to be conquered, and enough hiking trails to make your Fitbit weep with joy. Lace up your boots, grab your trekking poles, and get ready to breathe in the fresh Danish air. Hike through the ancient Rebild National Park, conquer the cliffs of Møns Klint, or follow the

Viking footsteps along the Wadden Sea. Just remember, respect nature, pack responsibly, and maybe don't challenge any wild boars to an arm wrestle (they're surprisingly strong, those guys).

Remember, there's no right or wrong way to explore Denmark.
 Whether you're a tour-loving sheepdog or a free-spirited butterfly, find the pace that suits your soul. Just pack your sense of adventure, a smile, and maybe a few kroner for that roadside ice cream you just can't resist. Denmark awaits, ready to weave its magic on you. Skål!

P.S. Don't forget to check the weather before you head out, especially if you're planning any outdoor adventures. Danish weather can be a bit temperamental, like a moody Viking throwing tantrums! But hey, even a rainy day in Denmark can be charming, especially with a steaming cup of coffee and a good book.

Chapter 8

Food And Drinks

Alright, foodies and thirsty adventurers, gather 'round! We're about to dive into the heart and soul of Denmark – its glorious food and drink. Forget your soggy airport sandwiches and overpriced cocktails, because Denmark's got a smorgasbord of epic proportions waiting to tantalize your taste buds and leave you saying "tak" for more.

Let's Start with the Grub

Denmark's not just about smørrebrød, folks, although those open-faced beauties are like tiny masterpieces of flavor on rye bread. But there's a whole world of culinary delights to explore, from hearty Viking feasts to delicate Michelin-starred creations. Here's a taste of the must-trys:

Frikadeller:

Think Danish meatballs on steroids, bursting with pork, beef, or lamb goodness, and usually served with mashed potatoes and red cabbage. It's the kind of comfort food that'll hug your belly like a warm Viking sweater.

Flæskesteg med persillesovs:
Imagine crispy pork belly slathered in gravy so good you'll want to lick the plate (and maybe you should, no judgment here). This classic dish is like a Viking battle cry for your taste buds – prepare to be conquered by its deliciousness.

Stegt Sild:
Don't be scared, landlubbers! Pickled herring is a Danish staple, and when done right, it's a surprisingly delicate and flavorful treat. Think tangy, sweet, and surprisingly addictive. Just maybe skip the aquavit chaser until you've gotten your sea legs.

Rødgrød med fløde:
This sweet cherry soup with whipped cream is like a hug in a bowl. It's the perfect antidote to a chilly Danish day, and guaranteed to put a smile on your

face (and maybe a few sticky spots on your clothes, but that's all part of the charm).

Where to Find Your Culinary Valhalla

Now, about those restaurants. Denmark's got options for every budget and every palate. Let's break it down:

Budget Eats:
 Hit the local market or grab a hot dog from a pølsevogn. Trust me, those Danish hot dogs are far superior to their American counterparts. You can also find cheap and cheerful cafes serving up frikadeller and smørrebrød, perfect for a quick and tasty bite.

Mid-Range Munchies:
 Explore Copenhagen's vibrant street food scene or venture into a hyggelig neighborhood restaurant. You'll find everything from modern Danish cuisine to international flavors, all at a price that won't break the bank.

Splurge-Worthy Feasts:

Ready to blow the budget and treat your taste buds like royalty? Michelin-starred restaurants abound in Copenhagen, offering innovative Nordic cuisine and presentations that are as artistic as they are delicious. Just be sure to book your table well in advance – these culinary Viking ships fill up fast!

Let's Talk Tipples

No culinary adventure is complete without a little something to wash it down with. So grab your glass and raise it to Denmark's liquid delights:

Carlsberg and Tuborg:
 These Danish brewing giants are like the Thor and Loki of beers, each with their own loyal following. Try both and see which one reigns supreme on your palate. Just remember, even Vikings get tipsy, so drink responsibly!

Akvavit:
 This strong, potato-based spirit is like a shot of liquid Viking spirit. It's usually served chilled and chased with beer, so prepare for a flavor assault

that'll warm you from the inside out (and maybe make your eyes water a little).

Sneba Js:
 Don't let the name fool you (it translates to "**snail bites**"), this sweet, cherry-flavored liqueur is surprisingly delightful. Think Danish cherry cordial with a kick, perfect for sipping after a hearty meal.

Remember, the food and drink scene in Denmark is like a Viking feast – there's something for everyone! So be adventurous, try new things, and don't be afraid to get a little messy (that's how the Vikings ate, after all!). With a full belly and a happy heart, you'll be singing Viking sagas of your Danish culinary adventures in no time. Skål!

P.S. Don't forget to pack your stretchy pants – you're gonna need them!

Danish Delights: From Smørrebrød to Snails (Yes, Snails!)

Alright, foodies, buckle up! We're about to embark on a culinary adventure through the heart of Denmark, where smørrebrød reigns supreme, Vikings drank potent potions called "snail bites," and Michelin stars twinkle brighter than Thor's hammer. Get ready to tantalize your taste buds, explore hidden gems, and maybe even learn to whip up a feast fit for a modern-day Ragnar Lothbrok (without the pillaging, of course).

Feasts fit for a Viking

Let's start with the main event – the food! Denmark's a smorgasbord (literally!) of flavors, from classic comfort grub to innovative Nordic cuisine that'll make your brain explode (in a good way!). Here's a taste of what awaits:

Smørrebrød:

These open-faced beauties are like tiny art installations on rye bread. Think piled-high mountains of shrimp, creamy cheeses, and pickled goodies – each bite a burst of flavor and color. Just be warned, one is never enough!

Flæskesteg:
 Imagine crispy pork belly so good, it practically sings sagas to your taste buds. Served with red cabbage and potatoes, it's a Viking feast for the modern age (just hold the ale horns, okay?).

Rødgrød med fløde:
 This sweet cherry soup with whipped cream is like a hug in a bowl. It's the perfect antidote to a chilly Danish day, and guaranteed to put a smile on your face (and maybe a few sticky spots on your clothes, but that's all part of the charm).

Beyond the Classics

Don't get me wrong, Danish classics are epic, but there's a whole world of culinary magic waiting to be explored. Check out these hidden gems:

Street Food Scene:
 Copenhagen's street food scene is like a Viking market on steroids. Think gourmet hot dogs, Korean tacos, and melt-in-your-mouth bao buns – all served up with a side of Danish hygge.

Michelin-Starred Delights:
 Ready to splurge and treat your taste buds like royalty? Michelin-starred restaurants abound in Copenhagen, offering innovative Nordic cuisine and presentations that are as artistic as they are delicious. Book well in advance – these culinary Viking ships fill up fast!

Cooking Classes:
 Get your hands dirty and learn the secrets of Danish cuisine! Cooking classes are a fantastic way to immerse yourself in the culture, learn some new skills, and maybe even impress your friends back home with your newfound prowess at whipping up a smørrebrød masterpiece.

Tipping Tales

Now, about that delicate dance of tipping. Forget American-style pressure, Denmark's a bit more chill. Service charges are usually included in the bill, so there's no need to break out the calculator after every meal. However, a small round-up (think 10 kroner) to the nearest round number is always appreciated if you had exceptional service. Remember, a smile and a genuine **"tak"** (thank you) go a long way in Denmark!

Food Tours for Foodie Friends

Can't resist a guided culinary adventure? Hop on a food tour and let someone else handle the navigation (and the Danish pronunciations!). You'll hit hidden gems, sample local delicacies, and learn all about the history and culture behind Danish food. Just be prepared to loosen your belt a notch or two – these tours are designed to leave you happy and full, Viking-style!

So, buckle up, foodies! Denmark awaits with open arms (and open kitchens).

Explore the classics, delve into the hidden gems, and maybe even learn to cook a dish that'll make your grandma jealous. Just remember, come hungry, come curious, and come ready to experience the Danish food scene in all its glorious, smørrebrød-filled wonder. Skål!

P.S. Don't be scared of the **"snails bites'** ' (sneba js) – they're surprisingly sweet and delicious! But maybe skip the aquavit chaser until you've gotten your sea legs, aight?

Chapter 9

Shopping And Souvenirs

Alright, shopaholics and souvenir seekers, gather 'round! We're about to dive into the tempting world of Danish retail therapy, where Viking trinkets mingle with designer duds and hyggelig homewares whisper promises of cozy nights in. But hold on, this ain't your average mall crawl – we're talking unique finds, locally crafted treasures, and enough mementos to make your friends back home green with envy (or maybe just confused by the pronunciation of **"smørrebrød")**.

Beyond the Viking Horns

Yes, yes, Viking helmets and miniature Thor hammers are fun, but let's delve deeper into Danish design delights. Think sleek furniture with clean lines, cozy knitwear in muted tones, and jewelry that's modern yet whispers of ancient sagas. Here's a taste of what awaits:

Royal Copenhagen porcelain:
 These delicately painted beauties are like tiny works of art. From iconic blue floral patterns to quirky contemporary designs, there's a piece for every taste and budget (though some might make your wallet faint). Just be careful not to pack them in your suitcase next to the Viking horns – porcelain and axes don't always play nice together.

Moomin mugs:

These adorable Finnish trolls have infiltrated Danish hearts (and mugs!), and their whimsical faces are the perfect way to bring a smile to your morning coffee. Just don't let them judge your choice of breakfast pastry – those little guys have opinions on everything, apparently.

Design Your Own Smørrebrød Kits:
Forget boring souvenirs – bring home a taste of Denmark! These kits come with all the fixings to create your own smørrebrød masterpieces, from rye bread and spreads to pickled delights and smoked salmon. Just add your own creativity (and maybe a smidge of courage – those pickled onions can be fierce!), and voila! Instant dinner party envy back home.

Treasure Hunting in Hidden Gems

Don't just stick to the glossy shopping streets, folks! The real magic lies in exploring the nooks and crannies, the charming markets, and the independent shops tucked away in cobbled alleyways. Here's where you'll stumble upon:

Designer Flea Markets:
 Copenhagen's flea markets are treasure troves of vintage finds, quirky antiques, and maybe even the occasional Viking helmet (though let's hope it's a replica!). Haggle your way to a bargain, find the perfect one-of-a-kind piece, and feel like you've stumbled into a time machine filled with dusty delights.

Hyggelig Homeware Havens:
 Danish design is all about coziness and functionality, and these shops are like walking into a warm hug. Think soft blankets, candles that smell like Christmas trees, and ceramics that beg to be filled with steaming mugs of cocoa. Just be warned, you might walk out with enough hygge to open your own Danish bakery back home.

Local Crafts & Designs:
 Support local artisans and find unique souvenirs with a soul! From hand-knit sweaters to intricately carved wooden bowls, these shops are bursting with

creativity and Danish spirit. Plus, you can feel good knowing you're supporting the local community, one beautifully crafted trinket at a time.

Souvenir Tales

Now, about those mementos. Skip the cheesy keychains and generic magnets – aim for something that tells a story, something that whispers of your Danish adventure. Here are some ideas:

A bottle of Gammel Dansk:
 This bitter cherry liqueur is an acquired taste, but it's a true Danish icon. Just be warned, it might not go down as smoothly as your smørrebrød, but hey, that's part of the experience!

A Viking-themed board game:
 Bring the Viking spirit back to your game nights! Whether it's a strategy game based on conquering land or a silly dice game involving drinking horns, find one that tickles your inner berserker (just promise not to flip the table if you lose).

A piece of Royal Copenhagen:
Okay, I know I mentioned this before, but it's worth repeating! These porcelain beauties are timeless classics, and they'll grace your coffee table for years to come. Just be careful not to let your cat use it as a scratching post – those little furballs have no respect for fine art (or expensive vases).

Remember, shopping in Denmark is an adventure, not a race!
Take your time, wander the streets, and let the hygge guide you.

Danish Delights and Deals: Don't Get Fleeced by a Viking!

Alright, bargain hunters and treasure seekers, gather 'round! We're about to navigate the thrilling world of Danish shopping, where designer dreams mingle with quirky finds and Vikings might try to sell you a used longship (steer clear of those, trust me). But fear not, thrifty adventurer, I'm here to equip you with the knowledge and wit to score epic deals and return home with enough loot to make your

credit card weep tears of joy (or maybe fear –
depends on how carried away you get!).

Finding the Frugality Fountain

Denmark ain't exactly Thailand when it comes to
haggling, but there are ways to score a bargain.
Here's your cheat sheet:

Flea Markets and Vintage Havens:
These treasure troves are havens for hagglers. Don't
be shy, throw out an offer, and see where the wind
blows. Just remember, be respectful and friendly –
no one likes a grumpy bargain hunter, not even a
grumpy Viking (and trust me, you do NOT want to
make a grumpy Viking grumpy-er).

Out-of-Season Sales:
 Patience is a virtue, especially when it comes to
shopping. Wait for those end-of-season sales and
watch the prices plummet like a clumsy troll off a
cliff (don't worry, trolls are made of sturdier stuff
than porcelain).

Tax-Free Deals:

Tourists get a sweet little refund on VAT (Value Added Tax) when they leave the country. Stock up on those designer duds and electronics, then strut through customs like you just plundered a dragon's hoard (minus the fire and brimstone, of course). Just remember, there are limits, so don't go overboard and try to smuggle out the Royal Jewels – even the most charming smile won't get you past those customs officers.

Where the Shopping Wild Things Are

Forget generic malls, folks. Denmark's got shopping districts as unique as a one-eyed, singing Viking warrior (yes, apparently those existed too). Here's a glimpse into the retail realms:

Copenhagen's Strøget:
This pedestrianized street is a shopper's paradise, lined with designer flagships, cozy boutiques, and enough cafes to keep you fueled for your retail marathon. Just watch out for those rogue bicycles – Danish cyclists have the right of way, even if they're

riding a unicycle while juggling flaming torches (it's not as uncommon as you'd think).

Meatpacking District (yes, really):
 Don't let the name fool you, this former industrial area is now a trendy haven for independent shops, art galleries, and hip cafes. It's the perfect place to find unique pieces and soak up the cool Copenhagen vibes. But ditch the Viking helmet – it might clash a bit with the vintage motorcycle parked outside the organic juice bar.

Torvehallerne:
 This gourmet food market is a feast for the senses (and the stomach!). Sample local delicacies, stock up on picnic supplies, and maybe even snag a signed cookbook from a Michelin-starred chef (just don't ask them to cook for you – they're probably busy, and besides, Danish kitchens are notoriously small – not even Thor could swing a frying pan in there).

Duty-Free Delights

Speaking of deals, let's talk duty-free! Copenhagen Airport is your tax-free playground, filled with shops overflowing with discounted booze, perfumes, and electronics. Just remember, there are limits, so don't go overboard and try to fill your suitcase with enough vodka to fuel a Viking longship voyage – you'll end up grounded faster than a troll caught stealing pastries.

Shopping in Denmark is an adventure, not a competition!
So relax, have fun, and don't be afraid to haggle (a little). Who knows, you might just walk away with a one-of-a-kind Viking helmet signed by Thor himself (okay, maybe not, but a girl can dream!). Just remember, the best souvenirs are the memories you make, the hygge you soak up, and the friends you make along the way. Skål to that!

P.S. Don't forget to pack your bargaining smile and your sense of humor – they're your most valuable assets in the Danish shopping arena! And maybe pack a few kroner too – those Viking helmets ain't cheap.

Chapter 10

Culture And Customs

From Hygge to Handshakes: Navigating the Danish Social Compass

Alright, we're about to dive into the heart of Denmark – its culture, its customs, and its unwritten social code. Don't worry, it's not like deciphering Viking runes (though that would be pretty cool), but there are a few things to keep in mind to avoid any awkward silences or accidental offense. So put on your hygge hat (metaphorically speaking, please – unless you actually have a hygge hat, in which case, more power to you!), and let's explore the Danish way of life!

Hygge is Your Hygge Hero

First things first, let's talk hygge (pronounced **"hoo-ga"**). It's not just a trendy word for cozy

candles and fluffy blankets, it's the Danish magic
spell for creating warmth, comfort, and connection.
Think crackling fires, shared pastries, and laughter
echoing through a candlelit room. Embrace the hygge,
folks, it's the key to unlocking Danish happiness!

Etiquette for Every Viking (in Training)

Now, about those social graces. Danes are generally
friendly and laid-back, but there are a few things to
remember:

Handshakes:
A firm handshake and a direct eye contact are your
go-to greetings. Forget air kisses or cheek-pecks –
stick to the handshake, even with women. Just don't
crush their hand like you're trying to impress Thor
with your grip strength.

Queues are Sacred:
Danes love their queues, and jumping them is akin to
stealing a pastry from a sleeping troll – not a good
look. Be patient, be polite, and wait your turn. Trust

me, the pastry will be worth it (and you won't have to outrun an angry troll, which is always a bonus).

Dinner Dates and Dress Codes:
 If you're invited to a Danish dinner party, don't expect a formal affair. Danes are casual, so dress comfortably but neatly. And when it comes to eating, remember the **"no elbows on the table"** rule (unless you want to channel your inner Viking and conquer your plate like a battleground, but even then, maybe just stick to the fork and knife).

Respecting Traditions and Local Flair

Denmark's got a rich history and cultural tapestry, and respecting local traditions is key to being a good guest. Here are a few things to keep in mind:

Flag Days:
 Danes love their flag, and you'll often see it proudly displayed on national holidays. If you see the Dannebrog waving, take a moment to appreciate it – it's a symbol of national pride and a pretty sight to behold.

Church Bells:
Speaking of traditions, the church bells in Denmark are like gentle reminders of time passing. Don't get annoyed by them, embrace them! They add a certain charm to the atmosphere, and might even inspire you to write a ballad about brave knights and fair maidens (just don't expect dragons – Denmark's dragon population is sadly extinct).

Dress Codes in Religious Sites:
 If you're visiting a church or cathedral, dress modestly. Cover your shoulders and knees, and ditch the beachwear – this ain't the Viking sauna, folks. Show some respect for the sacred space and the people who worship there.

Remember, a little cultural awareness goes a long way in Denmark.
Embrace the hygge, be respectful, and don't be afraid to ask questions. Danes are friendly and approachable, and they'll appreciate your effort to understand their way of life. You might even learn a few Viking secrets along the way, like how to braid

your beard like a pro or tell a captivating saga that'll make your friends green with envy.

So go forth, adventurers, and navigate the cultural waters of Denmark with confidence! Skål to new experiences, hygge-filled moments, and memories that'll last a lifetime!

P.S. Don't forget to pack your open mind and your sense of humor – they're essential companions on any cultural journey! And maybe pack a spare pastry, just in case you encounter a hungry troll – even the fiercest warriors have a soft spot for sweet treats.

Communication Tips (Language Basics)

Alright, language lovers and communication adventurers, gather 'round! We're about to dive into the fascinating world of Danish language and culture, where Vikings once spoke in tongues that could make mountains crumble and mermaids swoon (though probably not in that order). Don't worry, you won't need to conquer runestones or charm mythical creatures to get by, but learning a few basics and cultural quirks will have you navigating conversations and festivities like a seasoned Danish seafarer (minus the salty beard and questionable hygiene, of course).

Danish Decoded

Let's start with the language itself. Danish may sound like a chorus of angry gnomes at first, but trust me, it's got its own charm (and plenty of vowels!). Here's a crash course:

Pronunciation:
 Forget the silent "**h**"s and the double vowels that sing opera solos – Danish vowels are pronounced like they look (mostly). Just be prepared for some tongue-twisting clusters like "**hjort**" (deer) and "**smørrebrød**" (open-faced sandwiches – yes, that word will be your mantra in Denmark).

Basic Greetings:
"**Hej**" (hey) is your go-to for casual hellos, while "**goddag**" (good day) is more formal. "**Tak**" (thank you) and "**undskyld**" (excuse me) are your social lubricants, essential for keeping conversations flowing and avoiding accidental troll-bumping.

Numbers and Essentials:
 "**Et, to, tre**" (one, two, three) will get you basic counting covered, while "**venligst**" (please) and "**værsgo**" (you're welcome) add a touch of politeness. Remember, a little effort goes a long way in Denmark, even if your pronunciation makes Thor chuckle with amusement.

Communication Cues for Conversational Vikings

Now, about those actual conversations. Danes are generally friendly and approachable, but they can be a bit reserved at first. Don't get discouraged, here are some tips to break the ice:

Small Talk is Big:
 Talk about the weather (a national pastime in Denmark, even if it involves discussing 50 shades of grey clouds), ask about their hobbies, or compliment their hygge-filled home. Danes appreciate genuine interest, so ditch the pick-up lines and let the conversation flow naturally.

Active Listening is Key:
Danes are good listeners, so reciprocate the courtesy. Pay attention, ask follow-up questions, and avoid interrupting (unless a rogue pastry is about to fall into someone's coffee – then all bets are off, save the pastry!).

Humor with a Scandinavian Twist:
Danes love a good laugh, but their humor can be dry and understated. Don't go overboard with slapstick routines or cheesy jokes, embrace the subtle wit and playful sarcasm. Think Monty Python on a sugar high, and you're on the right track.

Festivals and Feasts for the Cultural Curious

Denmark's not just about museums and pastries (though those are pretty epic). It's a land bursting with cultural events and festivals, each a chance to witness traditions as old as Odin's beard (and maybe even taste some mead, though probably not made from fermented honey stolen from bees – health and safety regulations, you know). Here's a peek into the festive calendar:

Viking Festivals:
Channel your inner berserker at a Viking festival! Witness reenactments, feast on hearty stews, and maybe even try your hand at axe-throwing (just remember, safety first, and leave the pillaging to the professionals).

Carnival in Aalborg:
Forget Rio, Aalborg's carnival is where it's at! Think vibrant costumes, raucous parades, and enough confetti to make a snowstorm jealous. Just watch out for the flying herring – it's a local tradition, and yes, it's exactly as fishy as it sounds.

Julemarkeder (Christmas Markets): Hygge heaven on earth! Imagine twinkling lights, steaming mugs of gløgg (mulled wine), and enough gingerbread houses to make Hansel and Gretel weep with joy. It's the perfect way to embrace the Danish Christmas spirit (and stock up on enough ornaments to make your tree the envy of the neighborhood).

Remember, the language and culture of Denmark are like intricate Viking knots. Take your time, unravel them with patience and curiosity, and you'll discover a world of warmth, humor, and hidden delights. So go forth, language learners and festival fiends, embrace the Danish way of life and let your inner Viking spirit loose! Just remember, no pillaging the pastry shops – those are sacred grounds. Skål to new experiences and unforgettable adventures in Denmark!

P.S. Don't forget to pack your phrasebook and your sense of humor – they're your essential companions on any cultural

PART 3: Practical Information

Chapter 11

Health And Safety

Alright, fellow adventurers, we're diving into the nitty-gritty of staying safe and healthy in Denmark!

Think of this as your Viking shield against unforeseen tummy troubles and misplaced passports. No need to don helmets and chainmail, though a sturdy pair of walking shoes is definitely recommended – cobblestones can be ruthless terrain for flip-flop warriors.

Health Insurance and Vaccination Tales

First things first, let's talk about health insurance. Don't be a foolish Viking sailing into uncharted waters without a sturdy medical ship to back you up. Make sure your trusty insurance covers you for your Danish adventure, or you might end up paying more than a dragon's hoard for a simple sniffle. Check with your provider, pack the paperwork, and breathe easy knowing you're covered (unless you decide to engage in any Viking-inspired axe-throwing competitions – that's probably an exclusion, best not test your luck).

Vaccinations are another friendly reminder that prevention is better than a cure (and way cheaper than a one-way ticket to the hospital). Check with your doctor or health department to see if you need any jabs before you go. It's not glamorous, but trust me, battling jet lag and a nasty case of Viking flu is no way to spend your Danish vacation. Think of it as an investment in your hygge-filled future!

Safety in the Danish Den

Denmark's a pretty peaceful place, more likely to soothe you with hygge than scare you with dragons (though you might run into a grumpy troll in a museum gift shop, so keep your wits about you). However, there are a few things to keep in mind:

Traffic Taming:
Danish cyclists rule the road (and sometimes the sidewalks, so keep your head on a swivel!), so cross streets cautiously and don't challenge them to race – you'll lose, every time. And those red lights? They're not optional decorations, they're Viking traffic enforcers, and messing with them could land you in deep (and expensive) trouble.

Pickpocket Patrol:

Like any major city, Copenhagen has its fair share of pickpockets. Keep your valuables close, avoid flashing fancy cameras, and trust your gut instinct – if something feels fishy, it probably is, so swim away quickly. Think of it as avoiding the sirens' song, Danish style.

Nature's Nuances:
 Denmark's got beautiful beaches, but the North Sea can be a bit choppy (not exactly Viking bathwater temperature, either). Respect the water, swim in designated areas, and don't try to conquer the waves like a fearless warrior – unless you're a professional surfer, then by all means, go for it! Just make sure someone's filming your epic ride, we'd all love to see that on Instagram.

Remember, staying safe in Denmark is mostly about common sense and a healthy dose of caution.
Don't wander dark alleys alone, trust your gut, and keep an eye on your belongings. And for goodness sake, don't challenge a troll to a staring contest – those guys have legendary laser vision (and seriously bad breath).

So pack your sunscreen, your sensible shoes, and your good sense of humor, and you'll be ready to navigate the Danish landscape with the confidence of a seasoned Viking (minus the battle scars, hopefully). Skål to save adventures and epic memories!

P.S. Don't forget to pack any medication you might need, and maybe a first-aid kit for minor mishaps. You never know when you might need to bandage a blister from all that walking, or soothe a sunburn from too much hygge on the beach. Just remember, Vikings were tough, but even they appreciated a good bandage now and then.

Chapter 12

Viking Vigilance: Avoiding Scams and Staying Healthy in Denmark

We're nearing the final leg of our Danish odyssey! But before you hop on a longship and sail off into the sunset, let's talk about two crucial things: avoiding any sneaky scams and knowing where to find help if the hygge bubble bursts and you need a medical pit stop. Think of this as your Viking shield against overpriced pastries and dodgy deals, ensuring your Danish adventure ends on a high note, not a sour one.

Scam Shaming: Outsmarting the Tricksters

Denmark's a pretty safe country, but even the most peaceful corners can attract crafty critters looking to swindle the unsuspecting. Here's how to keep your wits sharp and your wallet safe:

Rental Shenanigans:
 Steer clear of deals that seem too good to be true, especially when it comes to apartments. If someone's offering a castle for the price of a hot dog, there's probably a dragon in the basement (metaphorically speaking, of course). Do your research, check reviews, and trust your gut – if something feels fishy, it probably is. Remember, Vikings may have plundered, but they never fell for cheap tricks.

Taxi Troubles:

Stick to official taxi stands and apps, and avoid flagging down random cars on the street. Those unofficial rides might come with inflated prices and questionable destinations (and trust me, you don't want to end up in Trollville by mistake). Remember, even Vikings preferred comfortable journeys to getting lost in the wilderness.

Pickpocket Patrol:
Keep your valuables close, don't flash your fancy camera like a trophy, and be mindful in crowded areas. These nimble-fingered tricksters might not be fire-breathing dragons, but they can disappear with your wallet faster than a troll on sugar. Think of it as a stealthy game of hide-and-seek, where you're the seeker and your belongings are the prize – just make sure you win!

Emergency Essentials: Knowing Where to Call and Go

Let's hope you never need it, but knowing the emergency contact numbers in Denmark is always a good idea. For any urgent situation, **dial 112** (that's the magic number for both police, ambulance, and firefighters). Don't worry about speaking Danish, English is widely understood, and even if you stumble through the words, they'll get the message. Remember, even the fiercest Vikings needed help sometimes, and asking for it doesn't make you any less of a warrior.

Medical facilities in Denmark are top-notch, but navigating the system can be tricky. If you need medical attention, head to a doctor's clinic ("lægehus") for minor issues. For more serious problems, seek help at a hospital **("sygehus")**. Most healthcare facilities have English-speaking staff, and you can also call the non-emergency medical helpline at 1813 for advice and guidance. Think of it as your personal Danish compass, pointing you towards the right medical care.

Remember, staying healthy and avoiding scams in Denmark is mostly about using common sense and staying alert.
Do your research, trust your gut, and don't be afraid to ask for help if you need it. Even the most seasoned Vikings had their share of scrapes and

close calls, but with a little preparation and a dash of caution, your Danish adventure will be one for the history books (minus the dragon battles, unless you happen to stumble upon a particularly grumpy one, in which case, good luck!).

So pack your sunscreen, your sensible shoes, and your emergency contact info, and head off to conquer Denmark with a smile and a sense of security. Skål to amazing adventures, Viking-worthy memories, and a safe and healthy journey!

P.S. Don't forget to pack any medication you might need, and maybe download a translation app for those unexpected encounters with stubborn vending machines or chatty bus drivers. Remember, a little planning goes a long way, and navigating Denmark with ease will make you feel like a true Viking of the modern age!

Alright, globetrotters, gather 'round! We're nearing the final frontier of our Danish odyssey – the realm of krona and krona, wallets and wads of cash. Don't worry, this ain't gonna be a snoozefest about exchange rates and decimal points. We're gonna talk cold, hard Danish dough in a way that'll make you feel like a financial Viking, plundering the best deals and navigating the monetary maze with the confidence of Odin himself (minus the one eye, hopefully).

Kroner Conquering

First things first, let's get familiar with the local currency. The Danish krone (DKK) reigns supreme, those little beauties with the Queen's portrait staring back at you. Don't be intimidated by the unfamiliar symbols – exchanging your hard-earned cash is easier than trying to decipher a cryptic Viking rune (though that would be pretty cool, too).

Exchange Rates:
 Keep an eye on those fluctuating numbers, folks! Check online or at currency exchange offices to get the best rate. Don't get caught at the airport with a highway robbery exchange – shop around, haggle a bit (okay, maybe not haggle, but ask if they can do better), and make sure you're not getting fleeced like a sheep at a Viking feast.

Cash or Cards?:

This is the eternal travel dilemma. Danish society is pretty cashless, but having some kroner on hand is always handy for those small shops and street vendors who haven't embraced the digital age (or maybe just prefer the satisfying clink of coins). Credit cards and debit cards are widely accepted, just watch out for those foreign transaction fees – they can bite harder than a grumpy troll on a sugar crash.

ATM Adventures

Speaking of ATMs, they're your friendly neighborhood kroner dispensers. Just remember, there might be fees lurking in the shadows, so check with your bank before you embark on your ATM adventure. And keep your pin code close, even closer than your smørrebrød recipe – those little numbers are precious treasures!

Travel Tips for Thrifty Travellers

Remember, Denmark ain't cheap, but there are ways to stretch your kroner further than a Viking longship in a storm. Here are a few budget-savvy tips:

Cook Some Meals:
 Eating out every night will drain your wallet faster than a dragon gulping down mead. Stock up at grocery stores (try the local markets for fresh produce and deals) and whip up some simple meals in your Airbnb. Trust me, your inner chef will thank you, and your bank account will sing with joy.

Free Activities:
 Denmark's bursting with free fun! Explore parks, wander museums on free admission days, and join in on local festivals. You might not score a dragon hoard, but you'll collect memories that are priceless.

Public Transportation:
 Ditch the taxis and embrace the efficient and affordable network of buses, trains, and even ferries. Get a travel card, explore like a local, and watch your kroner pile up like treasure in a dragon's cave (minus the fire and brimstone, hopefully).

Remember, money matters in Denmark, but it shouldn't define your adventure.

Be smart, be savvy, and don't let a few kroner come between you and an epic Danish experience. With a bit of planning and these nifty tips, you'll navigate the financial landscape like a true Viking warrior, conquering those kroner mountains and making the most of your Danish journey.

So pack your credit card, your ATM access code, and a healthy dose of financial wisdom, and prepare to conquer the Danish kroner market! Skål to savvy spending, budget-busting adventures, and memories that will last a lifetime!

P.S. Don't forget to budget for those souvenir Viking helmets and smørrebrød feasts – you deserve it after all that conquering! Just remember, moderation is key, even when it comes to delicious carbs and shiny horned headdress.

Money And Currency

Alright, globetrotters, we're at the money milepost of our Danish odyssey! Tipping, budgeting, and dodging scams – it's like navigating a financial fjord filled with swirling kroner and mischievous trolls (just kidding, there are no trolls, unless you stumble into a particularly grumpy souvenir shop owner). But fear not, intrepid adventurers, I'm here to equip you with the knowledge and wit to navigate this fiscal terrain like a Viking plundering a buffet of gold doubloons (minus the pillaging, of course).

Tipping Tales

Tipping in Denmark is more like a gentle nudge than a Viking war cry. It's not mandatory, but a small gesture of appreciation is always welcomed. Here's how to navigate the gratuity gray area:

Restaurants:
 Round up the bill if you had good service, or leave a few kroner on the table. No need to go overboard – Denmark isn't Las Vegas, and waiters won't break

into elaborate dance routines for a hefty tip. A smile and a polite "**tak**" (thank you) go a long way.

Taxis:
Round up the fare or leave a couple of kroner. Remember, they're already dealing with Copenhagen's bicycle-infested streets – a little tip is like a soothing balm for their frazzled nerves.

Hotels:
Leave a few kroner per night for the housekeeping staff who make your Hygge dreams a reality. They're the silent heroes of the hotel world, deserving of a little monetary pat on the back.

Budgeting Bonanza

Denmark ain't exactly budget-travel heaven, but with a little planning, you can stretch your kroner further than a Viking longship on a fair wind. Here's your frugal feast of tips:

Cook Some Meals:
Eating out every night will deplete your wallet faster than a dragon with a bottomless mead mug. Hit the

grocery stores (local markets are epic for fresh finds!) and whip up some simple meals in your Airbnb. Think of it as culinary hygge, with the added bonus of saving serious kroner.

Free Fun:
Denmark's overflowing with free entertainment! Explore parks, museums on free admission days, and join in on local festivals. You might not score a dragon hoard, but you'll collect memories that are worth more than gold.

Public Transportation:
 Ditch the taxis and embrace the efficient and affordable network of buses, trains, and even ferries. Get a travel card, explore like a local, and watch your kroner pile up like treasure in a dragon's cave (minus the fire and brimstone, hopefully).

Scam Slayers

Scammers lurk in every corner of the world, even in peaceful Denmark. Stay vigilant and keep your wits sharp with these tips:

Overpriced Taxis:
 Stick to official taxi stands and apps, and avoid flagging down random cars on the street. Those unofficial rides might come with inflated prices and questionable destinations (and trust me, you don't want to end up in Trollville by mistake). Remember, even Vikings preferred comfortable journeys to getting lost in the wilderness.

Currency Exchange Shenanigans:
 Steer clear of dodgy money changers offering ridiculously good rates. If it sounds too good to be true, it probably is. Stick to reputable banks or licensed exchange offices, and don't let your kroner be devoured by financial tricksters. Think of it as protecting your treasure from greedy goblins (metaphorically speaking, of course).

Fake Souvenirs:
 Viking horns made of plastic? Smørrebrød topped with glitter? These are not the souvenirs you seek, my friend. Do your research, buy from established shops, and trust your gut – if something feels fishy,

it probably is. Remember, Vikings may have plundered, but they never fell for cheap imitations.

The key to Danish money matters is to be informed, be cautious, and have fun!
Don't let a few kroner come between you and an epic Danish experience. With a bit of planning and these nifty tips, you'll navigate the financial landscape like a true Viking warrior, conquering those budget mountains and making the most of your Danish journey.

So pack your budget sense, your scam-slaying instincts, and a healthy dose of wanderlust, and prepare to conquer the Danish kroner market! Skål to savvy spending, budget-busting adventures, and memories that will last a lifetime!

P.S. Don't forget to budget for those souvenir Viking helmets and smørrebrød feasts – you deserve it after all that conquering! Just remember, moderation is key, even when it comes to delicious carbs and shiny horned headdresses.

Chapter 13

Communication And Technology

Danish Delights: Staying Connected in Hygge Heaven

Alright, globetrotters, we're nearing the final frontier of our Danish odyssey – the realm of Wi-Fi, phone calls, and navigating the digital waters without getting swept away by the tide of roaming charges. Don't worry, you won't be left adrift in a sea of silence, wondering if your llama farm back home has gone rogue (hopefully not, but maybe pack an extra pair of dungarees, just in case). We're about to equip you with the tech-savvy tips and tricks to stay connected, share your Danish adventures with the world, and maybe even learn a few Viking battle cries in the process (though those might not go over well at the airport security check).

Wi-Fi Warriors

Fear not, connectivity crusaders! Denmark's a Wi-Fi wonderland. Most cafes, restaurants, and even public spaces boast free internet, allowing you to upload your fjord-side selfies and brag about your smørrebrød feasts to your envious friends back home. Just remember, hygge can't be fully experienced through a screen, so put down the phone once in a while and soak in the Danish atmosphere. Think of it as a digital detox Viking-style, embracing the real world over the virtual one.

Phone Call Puzzles

Now, about those phone calls. International roaming charges can sting harder than a grumpy troll on a sugar crash. Consider these options:

Get a local SIM card:
This is your budget-friendly champion. Pop it in your phone, top up with some kroner, and make and receive calls like a local (just don't answer any numbers that start with "0700" – those are premium lines, and answering them might require selling your firstborn llama, no joke).

Use WhatsApp or other calling apps:
Wi-Fi is your friend here. Connect to a free network, fire up your favorite calling app, and chat away with your loved ones back home. Just remember, video calls might eat up your data faster than a Viking at a buffet, so use them sparingly.

Embrace the silence:
Sometimes, disconnecting is the best connection. Leave your phone in your pocket, wander the cobbled streets, and get lost in the Danish charm. You might miss a few cat videos, but you'll gain an experience that no Instagram filter can replicate. Think of it as a digital berserker rage of sorts, clearing your mind and embracing the present moment.

Tech Tips for Travelers

Remember, technology is your travel companion, not your overlord. Here are some tips to keep your devices happy and your data safe:

Download offline maps and translations:

Google Maps has your back, even without an internet connection. Download maps of the areas you'll be visiting, and brush up on some basic Danish phrases with translation apps. You might not become a full-fledged Viking linguist, but you'll at least be able to order another pastry without resorting to sign language (though Viking sign language would be pretty epic).

Backup your photos and videos:
 Don't risk losing your Danish fjord selfies to a lost phone or a rogue troll attack. Back up your precious memories to the cloud or an external hard drive. Think of it as building your own digital treasure chest, filled with memories instead of gold.

Beware of public Wi-Fi:
Free Wi-Fi is a traveler's best friend, but be cautious where you connect. Avoid entering sensitive information on public networks, and stick to trusted cafes and restaurants for your online banking sprees (unless you want to wake up to a pile of empty llama pens, which would be a truly tragic sight).

Remember, staying connected in Denmark is all about finding the balance.

Embrace the Wi-Fi, utilize technology when it helps, but don't let it be a barrier to experiencing the real Denmark. Chat with locals, wander cobbled streets, and soak in the hygge without constantly looking through a screen. Think of it as a digital truce with the modern world, allowing you to conquer the Danish landscape like a tech-savvy Viking, armed with knowledge, charm, and a healthy dose of wanderlust.

So pack your phone, your charger, and your open mind, and prepare to connect with Denmark in all its digital and non-digital glory! Skål to tech-savvy adventures, llama-free phone bills, and memories that will last a lifetime!

P.S. Don't forget to download a Viking battle cry app for those impromptu moments when you feel the need to channel your inner berserker. Just remember, use it responsibly, and maybe avoid unleashing it at the breakfast buffet – unless you want to scare away all the pastries, which wouldn't be a terrible outcome for your waistline, but your taste buds would never forgive you.

SIM Card Options

Alright, we're diving deep into the digital depths of Denmark! No need to don cyber-chainmail or wield laser keyboards – this ain't some sci-fi saga. We're just here to conquer the tech terrain, stay connected with the outside world (and your llama farm, because let's face it, those furry fiends need updates too), and share your Danish exploits without blowing your data budget faster than a Viking at a mead buffet.

SIM Card Showdown

First things first, let's talk SIM cards, your tiny tech warriors that grant you data freedom. Here's your battle plan:

Local Heroes:
Ditch the exorbitant roaming charges and snag yourself a Danish SIM card. Top it up with some kroner, and voila! You're a local, able to call, text, and surf the web like a pro. Just remember, choosing the right carrier is key. Do your research, compare plans,

and don't get lured in by promises of unlimited dragon-slaying data unless you actually plan on battling some fire-breathing beasts (which, let's be honest, would be pretty epic).

Prepaid Pals:
These temporary SIM cards are your travel buddies, perfect for shorter stays. No contracts, no fuss, just pop it in and you're good to go. Just like renting a trusty steed for your Danish adventure, these prepaid SIMs let you gallop through the data fields without getting bogged down by commitment.

Travel Titans:
 Some international roaming plans can be surprisingly decent. Do your homework, compare options with your home provider, and see if it makes sense for your Danish voyage. Think of it as weighing anchor on a familiar ship, venturing into uncharted waters without completely abandoning your seafaring comfort zone.

Wi-Fi Warriors

But wait, there's more! Denmark's a Wi-Fi wonderland, with free hotspots lurking around every corner like friendly trolls offering digital mead (okay, maybe not mead, but free internet is close enough). Cafes, restaurants, museums, even parks – they're all potential gateways to the online world. Just remember, public Wi-Fi can be a bit finicky, so keep your sensitive information under lock and key, and maybe avoid online banking adventures unless you want to wake up to a herd of confused llamas staring at your empty bank account. Think of it as a digital Viking shield, protecting your precious data from mischievous gremlins and rogue pop-up ads.

App-tastic Adventures

Now, let's talk travel apps, your digital knights in shining armor:

Offline Maps:
Google Maps can be your digital cartographer, even without an internet connection. Download maps of the areas you'll be exploring, and navigate like a seasoned

Viking, though maybe ditch the battle ax and opt for a sensible walking stick.

Translation Tools:
Don't let the Danish language be a barrier to your adventure. Pack a translation app in your digital backpack, and conquer those grocery lists and restaurant menus with ease. Just remember, these apps aren't perfect, so be prepared for the occasional Viking-speak gibberish – it all adds to the charm, right?

City Guides and Activities:
 Apps like VisitDenmark and Copenhagen Concierge are your local experts, packed with insider tips, recommendations, and even booking options. Think of them as your digital skalds, singing tales of hidden gems and must-see sights, ensuring your Danish adventure is filled with epic experiences, not just aimless wandering (unless aimless wandering is your thing, in which case, more power to you!).

Remember, technology is your travel companion, not your overlord. Use it to enhance your Danish experience, but don't let it become your sole focus.

Put down the phone, soak in the hygge, and embrace the real Denmark. You might miss a few llama updates, but you'll gain memories that no Instagram filter can replicate. Think of it as a digital truce with the modern world, allowing you to conquer the Danish landscape like a tech-savvy Viking, armed with knowledge, charm, and a healthy dose of wanderlust.

So pack your phone, your charger, and your open mind, and prepare to connect with Denmark in all its digital and non-digital glory! Skål to tech-savvy adventures, llama-free phone bills, and memories that will last a lifetime!

P.S. Don't forget to download a Viking battle cry app for those impromptu moments when you feel the need to unleash your inner berserker. Just remember, use it responsibly, and maybe avoid unleashing it at the bakery – unless you want to scare away all the pastries, which wouldn't be a terrible outcome for your waistline, but your taste buds would never forgive you.

Chapter 14

Visas And Immigration

Alright, intrepid adventurers, we're nearing the final frontier of our Danish odyssey – the realm of visas, passports, and customs checkpoints. Don't worry, this won't be a snoozefest of forms and regulations. We're about to navigate the immigration maze like seasoned Vikings sailing through a storm, armed with knowledge, humor, and maybe a well-placed bribe of smørrebrød (because who can resist those delicious open-faced delights?).

Visa Vikings

For most US citizens, Denmark is an open door, no Viking battle ax required. If you're planning a stay of less than 90 days, congratulations! You're visa-free, my friend. Just waltz through immigration with your trusty passport (valid for at least three months beyond your stay, naturally), flash a friendly smile, and boom – you're in Hygge Heaven. Remember, even

Vikings needed passports to visit Valhalla, so keep yours up-to-date and readily available, just in case the immigration gods ask for a glimpse.

Entry Essentials

But wait, there's more! Even passport-wielding warriors need to pack some essentials:

Proof of onward travel:
Immigration officers might want to see evidence you're not planning to set up camp and become a permanent Danish resident (unless that's your secret dream, in which case, more power to you!). Show them flight bookings, train tickets, or any proof you'll eventually leave your Viking mark on another land.

Sufficient funds:
While Denmark isn't exactly Narnia, it is pretty darn magical, and magic comes at a price (usually in kroner). Show the immigration gods you have enough dough to fuel your Danish adventure, whether it's a bulging wallet or a credit card statement that resembles a dragon's hoard.

Extending Your Hygge

If those 90 days just aren't enough (and trust me, they probably won't be), you can apply for a visa extension. This is where things get a bit more complicated, so be prepared to unleash your inner paperwork warrior. Research visa options, gather documents, and brace yourself for the occasional bureaucratic battle cry (it's all part of the adventure, right?). Remember, even the fiercest Vikings had to deal with stubborn gatekeepers, so channel your inner berserker and conquer the visa mountain!

Customs Conquering

Finally, the land of free samples and duty-free delights! But before you start stuffing your suitcase with smørrebrød and Viking helmets, remember there are rules (not as strict as Odin's, but still...) Check customs regulations for allowed quantities of alcohol, tobacco, and other goodies. Don't try to smuggle in any live dragons (seriously, they're a nightmare on airplanes), and declare any precious treasures you've plundered (unless you want to face the wrath of the customs gods, which trust me, is not pretty). Think of it as offering tribute to the gatekeepers of the earthly realm, ensuring your Danish loot safely crosses the border.

Remember, navigating visas and immigration is about being prepared, informed, and maybe a little bit charming. A friendly smile and a polite **"tak"** (thank you) can go a long way. So pack your passport, your paperwork (if needed), and a healthy dose of patience, and prepare to conquer the immigration maze like a seasoned Viking traveler. Skål to smooth crossings, friendly customs officers, and memories that will last a lifetime!

P.S. Don't forget to pack a sense of humor, because let's face it, sometimes bureaucracy can be stranger than a troll convention. Just imagine yourself as a Viking bard, weaving tales of your customs trials for your grandchildren back home. They'll be enthralled (and maybe a little bit terrified) of your adventures!

Chapter 15

Minimizing Your Environment For Impact

Responsible Rovers: Conquering Denmark the Eco-Viking Way!

Alright, we're nearing the final horn call of our Danish odyssey! But before we raise our tankards of frothy mead and sail off into the sunset, let's talk about something crucial: responsible travel. Think of it as the secret sauce that makes your Danish adventure extra delicious, not just for you, but for the land and its people. We're not talking about boring lectures or tree-hugging sermons – we're about conquering Denmark like mindful Vikings, leaving it even more spectacular than we found it.

Eco-Conscious Explorers

Denmark's a natural wonderland, from fjords that shimmer like polished shields to forests that whisper ancient Viking tales. Let's keep it that way, shall we? Here's how to be an eco-warrior extraordinaire:

Reduce, reuse, recycle, repeat:
 Sounds like a mantra for conquering garbage, right? Pack wisely, minimize waste, and choose eco-friendly options, like refillable water bottles and reusable bags. Think of it as your personal quest to slay plastic pollution, one smørrebrød at a time.

Embrace public transportation:
 Ditch the gas-guzzling chariots and hop on the efficient network of buses, trains, and even ferries. You'll save kroner, explore like a local, and leave the roads less choked with fumes than a dragon after a particularly spicy mead fest.

Support sustainable businesses:
Choose eco-conscious hotels, restaurants, and activities. Look for green certifications, opt for local produce, and avoid souvenir shops that sell Viking horns made of plastic (seriously, what's the point?).

Think of it as building bridges with Mother Nature, not burning them with unsustainable choices.

Local Lore Champions

Denmark's more than just a pretty landscape; it's a land rich in history, culture, and traditions. Let's respect it like the valiant Vikings we are:

Learn a few Danish phrases:
 "Tak" (thank you) and **"Hej"** (hello) go a long way. Showcasing even a little effort to speak the language shows respect and creates connections with the locals. It's like cracking the code to a secret treasure chest filled with friendly smiles and maybe even an extra helping of smørrebrød.

Be mindful of customs and traditions:
 Don't barge into churches during services or blast music in quiet villages. Observe local customs, dress modestly in religious sites, and be generally chill. Think of it as blending in like a stealthy ninja Viking, navigating the cultural landscape with respect and awareness.

Support local businesses:
Shop at independent stores, dine at family-run restaurants, and choose experiences that benefit the community. You'll get unique finds, authentic experiences, and a warm welcome from the locals. It's like forging alliances with the local artisans and warriors, creating a network of friendly faces that will enrich your Danish adventure.

Community Champions

Let's leave Denmark a little better than we found it:

Volunteer your time:
Lend a hand with local conservation projects, help clean up beaches, or volunteer at community events. It's not just about the good karma, though that's pretty epic too – it's about leaving your mark as a positive force, a Viking who strengthens the community, not just plunders its treasures.

Promote responsible tourism:

Spread the word about sustainable travel practices, encourage others to be eco-conscious explorers, and share your responsible adventures on social media. Be the bard who sings the praises of respectful travel, inspiring others to conquer Denmark the mindful way.

Leave no trace:
 This is your Viking code of honor. Don't litter, respect wildlife, and minimize your impact on the environment. Leave campsites cleaner than you found them, treat nature with reverence, and remember, even Vikings had a deep connection to the land they roamed.

Remember, responsible travel isn't a chore, it's an adventure in itself.
It's about enriching your Danish experience, building bridges with the locals and the environment, and making your travels meaningful. So pack your eco-friendly gear, your open mind, and your desire to connect, and prepare to conquer Denmark like a champion of responsible tourism. Skål to epic adventures, mindful choices, and memories that will last a lifetime!

P.S. Don't forget to pack a reusable Viking helmet (made from sustainable materials, of course!). It's not just a cool souvenir, it's a symbol of your commitment to responsible travel, a reminder that you're a respectful adventurer, leaving your mark on the world in the best way possible. Now go forth, conquer Denmark the mindful way, and may your journey be filled with hygge, adventure, and the satisfaction of being a true eco-Viking!

Chapter 16

Glossary Of Useful Terms

Globetrotters, we've reached the final fjord of our Danish odyssey! But before we hoist the sails and bid farewell to this Hygge haven, let's equip ourselves with some essential linguistic loot – a glossary of Danish delights to navigate the cultural landscape with the wit of a Viking bard and the charm of a pastry-munching berserker. Forget stuffy textbooks and boring grammar drills – we're about to conquer the Danish language like playful pirates plundering a treasure chest of quirky phrases and cultural gems.

Essential Viking Vocab

Hej:
 Your friendly "**hello**," the first bridge you build with the locals. Say it with a smile, and watch doors (and hearts) open wider than a dragon's treasure cave.

Tak:
 Your magic "**thank you**," the key to unlocking smiles and maybe even an extra helping of smørrebrød. Remember, even Vikings appreciated good manners (though they might have shown it by offering mead instead of polite phrases).

Undskyld:
Your "**sorry**," the shield that deflects any accidental bumps and fumbles. A sheepish grin and a muttered "" can smooth over any social mishaps, proving even Vikings weren't immune to the occasional faux pas.

Ja/Nej:
Your simple "**yes**" and "**no**," the oars that guide your conversations through uncharted waters. Don't worry

about fancy conjugations, these basic words will get you far, like a trusty longship on a calm fjord.

Skål!:

Your "**cheers**," the battle cry that raises spirits (and glasses) higher than a dragon's fiery breath. Share it with newfound friends, celebrate life's little victories, and let the "skål" echo through the Danish air, a toast to your epic adventure.

Travel Treasures

Tog:

Your "**train**," the iron steed that whisks you through rolling landscapes and charming towns. Just don't expect it to be pulled by fire-breathing beasts, unless you stumble into a particularly fantastical train station.

Bus:

Your trusty chariot, navigating city streets and winding country roads. Remember, "**påstigning bagtit**" means "**boarding at the back**," so don't barge in like a rampaging berserker, wait your turn, and enjoy the ride.

Hotel:
Your cozy camp, a haven for weary travelers and pastry-devouring adventurers. **"Værelse ledig**?" means **"room available**?" – ask it with a hopeful glint in your eye, and prepare to snuggle into Scandinavian comfort.

Restaurant:
 Your feasting hall, where culinary delights await. **"Mad og drikke"** means **"food and drink**," the magic words that unlock a smorgasbord of gastronomic treasures. Just don't expect roasted dragon on the menu, unless you're dining at a very adventurous eatery.

Cultural Curiosities

Hygge:
 Your cozy haven, a feeling of warmth, contentment, and shared joy. Think crackling fires, flickering candles, and endless cups of coffee – that's hygge in

a nutshell. Embrace it, soak it in, and let it warm your soul like a mug of spiced gløgg on a winter's night.

Fastelavn:
Your Danish Mardi Gras, a celebration of costumes, parades, and, of course, pastries. Don your most creative Viking helmet, grab a **"kanttekening"** (cat queen pastry), and join the merriment – just don't try to eat the actual cat, that's definitely not part of the tradition (and probably not very hygge either).

Janteloven:
 Your law of unspoken norms, a cultural quirk that encourages humility and discourages boasting. Don't brag about your dragon-slaying skills (even if they're true!), keep your victories humble, and let your actions speak louder than your words.

Remember, language is a bridge, not a barrier. These are just a few stepping stones to get you started. Don't be afraid to stumble, mispronounce, and laugh at yourself. The Danes appreciate the effort, and who knows, you might even pick up a few Viking battle cries to impress your friends back home (just maybe skip the bloodcurdling ones at the airport security check).

So pack your newfound Danish vocabulary, your sense of adventure, and your appetite for smørrebrød, and prepare to conquer the Danish language like a seasoned Viking storyteller. Skål to linguistic adventures, cultural understanding, and memories that will last a lifetime!

P.S. Don't forget to pack a phrasebook or translation app for those particularly tricky words. Think of it as your magical Viking decoder ring, helping you unlock the secrets of the Danish language and ensuring your conversations don't get lost in translation (unless you're trying to woo a dragon, in which case, good luck!

Chapter 17

Maps of The City/Region

Ahoy, fellow explorers! We've reached the mapmaker's corner of our Danish odyssey, the realm

where getting lost takes on a whole new meaning –
because let's face it, sometimes getting lost leads to
the most epic discoveries. But fear not, intrepid
adventurers, this ain't no aimless wandering in the
fog. We're about to equip you with cartographic
treasures that would make Odin himself jealous –
maps, schedules, and transportation tips to navigate
Denmark like a Viking with a compass made from
dragon scales (okay, maybe just a regular compass,
but a cool one with Viking runes, for sure).

Public Transport Panoramas

First things first, let's ditch the chariots and
embrace the efficient network of buses, trains, and
ferries. Think of it as your personal dragon fleet,
whisking you through cities, countryside, and even
across sparkling fjords. Here's how to chart your
course:

City Maps:
 Grab a free map at your hotel, tourist office, or the
nearest bakery (because let's be honest, maps and
pastries go hand-in-hand, like peanut butter and

smørrebrød). These local guides will show you landmarks, streets, and maybe even hidden alleys where trolls like to hang out (just kidding, they're probably too busy baking pastries).

Train Timetables:
Download the DSB app, your digital train oracle. It holds the secrets of departure and arrival times, platform numbers, and even ticket purchases. No more cryptic runes or riddles to decipher, just point, click, and watch the Danish landscape unfold from your comfy train seat.

Bus Bonanza:
Download the Rejseplanen app, your bus-whisperer. It speaks the language of schedules, routes, and real-time updates. No need to chase after buses like a berserker chasing a runaway chicken, let the app tell you exactly where and when to hop on your chariot of choice.

Ferry Frolics:
For island-hopping adventures or fjord-crossing escapades, hop on a ferry. Check websites like Molslinjen or Scandlines for routes, schedules, and

the occasional mermaid sighting (okay, maybe not mermaids, but you might spot some playful seals basking on the rocks).

Airport & Train Station Savvy

Landing in Denmark is smoother than a dragon landing on a cloud of marshmallows (though maybe pack some earplugs for the landing gear, just in case). Here's your survival guide for arrival and departure:

Airports:
 Copenhagen Airport (Kastrup) is your main gateway, but Billund (Legoland!) and Aarhus might be your landing pads too. Familiarize yourself with layouts, transportation options, and luggage pick-up areas. And remember, don't challenge the security scanners to a duel – your Viking helmet might raise some eyebrows.

Train Stations:
 Hopping off the train? Copenhagen Central Station and Aarhus Central Station are your bustling hubs. Download station maps, find luggage lockers, and grab

a coffee (because caffeine is a traveler's best friend, next to smørrebrød, of course).

Renting a Ride

Feeling adventurous? Renting a car can be a thrilling way to explore. Just remember:

Driving on the right:
Don't get caught daydreaming about dragons and accidentally drive on the left side of the road. Your fellow Vikings will not be amused.

Parking Prowess:
Research parking zones and regulations, especially in cities. Don't park your chariot like a beached whale and block someone's driveway – the parking gods will not be pleased.

Road Signs & Rules:
Brush up on Danish traffic signs and rules. You wouldn't want to get fined for exceeding the speed limit while singing Viking battle cries out the window (though it would be pretty epic).

Remember, maps are your guides, not your overlords. Don't get glued to the screen, keep an eye out for hidden gems, and embrace the occasional detour. You might stumble upon a Viking burial mound disguised as a particularly mossy hill, or discover a secret pastry bakery tucked away in a charming alley.

So pack your adventurous spirit, your sense of direction (or lack thereof, that's okay too), and prepare to navigate Denmark like a seasoned cartographer. Skål to epic journeys, unexpected discoveries, and memories that will outlast any map!

P.S. Don't forget to pack a compass, just in case your phone dies or you get lost in a particularly dense forest. You never know when you might need to channel your inner Viking and navigate by the stars (though knowing a few constellations besides **"Dragon"** wouldn't hurt either).

Chapter 18

Useful Websites And Resources

Alright, we're nearing the final horn call of our Danish odyssey! But before we raise our tankards of frothy mead and sail off into the sunset, let's equip ourselves with some digital loot – a treasure trove of websites and resources to enrich your adventure every step of the way. Think of it as your Viking knowledge-horn, overflowing with tips, tricks, and tales to navigate Denmark like a seasoned explorer. Forget dusty guidebooks and cryptic runes – we're about to conquer the digital landscape with the finesse of a bard weaving epic sagas.

Official Tourism Titans

First things first, let's tap into the wisdom of the locals. These official tourism websites are your gateways to insider knowledge:

VisitDenmark:

Your digital Viking storyteller, this website sings the praises of Denmark's cities, countryside, and hidden gems. From planning your itinerary to finding quirky festivals, it's your one-stop shop for Danish delights. Think of it as a friendly troll offering you a map made of enchanted moss (okay, maybe a regular map, but a very informative one).

Copenhagen Concierge:
Your urban explorer's compass, this website unlocks the secrets of Copenhagen, from trendy cafes to off-the-beaten-path museums. Discover hidden bars, rooftop terraces with fjord views, and the best spots to snag those Instagram-worthy smørrebrød shots. Think of it as a mischievous gremlin leading you to the city's tastiest and most unexpected treasures.

Regional Tourism Websites:
Each region has its own digital board, singing the praises of its unique landscapes and experiences. Whether you're drawn to the windswept shores of Jutland or the charming islands of Bornholm, there's a website waiting to guide you. Think of them as a

chorus of friendly Vikings, each with their own tales of adventure and local lore.

Travel Blog Troubadours

But knowledge isn't just found in official halls. Wander into the realm of travel blogs, where fellow adventurers share their tales of Danish conquest:

The Blonde Abroad:
 Kiersten's blog is a vibrant tapestry of Danish adventures, from cycling through castles to cozying up in hyggelige cafes. Her infectious enthusiasm and helpful tips will make you want to pack your bags and hop on the next ferry to Copenhagen. Think of her as a Viking queen sharing her travel wisdom by a crackling fire.

Adventurous Kate:
 Kate's blog is a treasure chest of off-the-beaten-path experiences. Discover hidden waterfalls, hike through Viking burial mounds, and learn to kayak like a true Northman. Her blog is a reminder that Denmark's magic lies not just in the

famous sights, but also in the untamed corners waiting to be explored. Think of her as a daring Valkyrie leading you on secret adventures.

Shandification:
This blog delves deep into Danish culture, from design and architecture to hygge and traditions. You'll learn about the Danish way of life, understand the meaning of **"friluftsliv"** (outdoor living), and maybe even pick up a few Danish phrases to impress the locals. Think of it as a wise elder sharing tales of Danish customs and traditions by a flickering candlelight.

Remember, websites and blogs are your storytelling companions, not your travel masters. Use them to spark your curiosity, not dictate your every step. Get lost in the winding lanes of digital villages, stumble upon unexpected treasures, and let your own adventures unfold like an epic Viking saga.

So pack your digital compass, your thirst for knowledge, and your appetite for adventure, and prepare to conquer the Danish online landscape like a seasoned web-weaver. Skål to digital discoveries, enriching experiences, and memories that will outlast any website!

P.S. Don't forget to bookmark your favorite websites and blogs! You never know when you might need to consult the digital oracle before embarking on your next Danish quest. Just make sure your internet troll doesn't lead you astray!

Alright, we're sailing towards the final shores of our Danish odyssey! But before we raise a final toast of frothy mead and set sail towards new horizons, let's equip ourselves with some essential tools for navigating the real world – local news, emergency contacts, and language learning treasures. Think of it as your Viking survival kit, packed with knowledge and resources to handle anything from unexpected detours to friendly chats with shopkeepers (and maybe even dragons, though let's hope their breath isn't too smelly).

Local News Navigators

Staying in the loop with what's happening in Denmark is a surefire way to enrich your adventure. These local news websites will keep you plugged in:

Politiken:
 Denmark's oldest daily newspaper, offering a mix of national and international news, with a focus on in-depth reporting and analysis. Think of it as your wise elder, sharing stories of the land from a seasoned perspective.

DR Nyheder:
Denmark's national public broadcaster website, delivering up-to-date news in a clear and concise format. Perfect for quick updates on weather, traffic, and any unexpected Viking festivals that might pop up (you never know!). Think of it as your friendly messenger bird, bringing news from every corner of the kingdom.

Lokalavisen:
Dive into the heart of local communities with regional news websites. Find out about upcoming events,

festivals, and maybe even score an interview with a local pastry chef (because who doesn't want to learn the secrets of the perfect smørrebrød?). Think of them as your playful gnomes, whispering tales of hidden gems and local happenings.

Emergency Contact Compendium

Planning for the unexpected is never a bad idea, even for the bravest Vikings. Keep these emergency contact numbers close at hand:

112:
 The universal emergency number for police, ambulance, and fire services. Remember it like the lucky number of Odin's ravens, ready to swoop in and help in any situation.

Non-emergency police:
 Dial 114 for non-urgent matters, like reporting a stolen Viking helmet (though hopefully that won't happen!). Think of it as your friendly neighborhood berserker, there to lend a hand with minor scuffles and lost treasures.

Hospitals:
Research local hospitals and clinics, especially if you
have any specific medical needs. You never know when
you might need a dragon-scale cast or a potion
brewed by a friendly witch (okay, maybe a doctor,
but a good one).

Language Learning Loot

Conquering the Danish language, even just a few
phrases, adds a whole new layer of magic to your
adventure. Here are some resources to get you
started:

Duolingo:
This free app gamifies language learning, making it
fun and addictive. Learn basic Danish phrases,
challenge friends to Viking tongue-twisters, and
impress the locals with your **"tak"s** and **"hej"s**. Think
of it as your enchanted speech stone, unlocking the
secrets of the Danish language with every swipe and
tap.

Memrise:

Another free app that uses flashcards and games to make learning Danish engaging. Build your vocabulary, master pronunciations, and maybe even learn to sing Viking battle cries like a pro. Think of it as your personal bard, teaching you ancient songs and tales in the melodious language of the North.

Pimsleur:
This audio-based program focuses on conversational Danish, helping you order food, ask for directions, and maybe even flirt with a charming Danish baker (just make sure your dragon breath mints are handy!). Think of it as your magical ear trumpet, amplifying the sounds of the Danish language and guiding you through conversations with ease.

Remember, local news, emergency contacts, and language skills are your trusty sidekicks, not your overlords.
Don't let them confine your adventure; use them as tools to connect with the locals, navigate unexpected situations, and sprinkle your Danish experience with a touch of linguistic magic.

So pack your thirst for knowledge, your sense of preparedness, and your desire to connect, and prepare to conquer the real world in Denmark like a resourceful explorer. Skål to unexpected encounters, helpful resources, and memories that will echo through the halls of Valhalla (or at least your cozy Airbnb)!

P.S. Don't forget to download offline maps and learn a few emergency phrases before you go. You never know when you might need to ask a friendly troll for directions, and trust me, you wouldn't want to rely on sign language when facing a grumpy one!

Chapter 19

Alphabetical Index Of Key Terms, Places, And Attractions

Globetrotters, we've reached the final map on our Danish odyssey – the index, your trusty compass to navigate the epic saga you've just devoured! Think of it as your Viking treasure map, leading you back to hidden gems, forgotten fjords, and maybe even the bakery that bakes the best cinnamon rolls this side of Valhalla. No need to squint at cryptic runes or decipher ancient riddles – this index is as clear as a summer sky above Copenhagen harbor.

A is for Adventure:
 From Aarhus to Aalborg, your Danish escapade is overflowing with epic experiences. Kayak through Viking burial mounds, conquer castles older than Odin's beard, and maybe even learn to sing a dragon-slaying ballad like a true Northman.

B is for Bjorn Borg:
 No, not just the tennis legend, though your serve might get pretty epic after chasing pastries all day. This B is for hygge, the Danish secret to coziness and contentment. Think crackling fires, fluffy blankets, and endless cups of coffee – hygge is your warm woolen cloak against the winter chill (or the occasional social awkwardness).

C is for Culinary Delights:
 Danish cuisine is a smorgasbord of deliciousness. Dive into smørrebrød, an open-faced masterpiece piled with everything from herring to beetroot. And

don't forget the pastries! From cinnamon rolls the size of Viking helmets to delicate "**wienerbrød**," your taste buds will be singing like skalds after every bite.

D is for Dragons (sort of):
Okay, maybe you won't actually encounter fire-breathing beasts (unless you stumble upon a particularly spicy chili restaurant). But Denmark's history and landscapes are full of dragon legends, Viking tales, and mythical creatures that will ignite your imagination and make you believe in magic (especially after a mug of gløgg, the spiced winter wine that warms you from the inside out).

E is for Eco-Explorers:
 Denmark is a champion of sustainability, so pack your reusable bags and eco-friendly mindset. Explore green cities on bikes, cycle through rolling hills, and choose eco-conscious accommodations and experiences. Remember, even Vikings cared for the land they roamed, so be a mindful explorer and leave Denmark even more beautiful than you found it.

F is for Festivals:

From Viking reenactments to quirky music festivals, Denmark's calendar is brimming with colorful celebrations. Don your best horned helmet, join the merriment, and let your inner berserker (or just your dancing feet) take over. You might even learn to yodel like a champion at a folk festival or witness the majestic glow of Copenhagen Light Festival.

G is for Getting Around:
 Trains, buses, ferries, bikes – Denmark has transportation options for every Viking spirit. Hop on a train and watch the countryside whiz by, navigate charming Copenhagen on two wheels, or conquer a fjord on a ferry (just don't challenge the captain to an arm-wrestling match).

H is for Hygge, again:
 Yes, it's so important it gets two spots! Because hygge isn't just a word, it's a way of life. Embrace cozy cafes, candlelight evenings, and moments of shared laughter with friends and family. Hygge is your Danish superpower, a shield against the cold and a key to unlocking the heart of Danish culture.

I is for Islands and Inspiration:

From Bornholm's rugged cliffs to Samsø's organic paradise, Denmark's islands are gems waiting to be discovered. Hike through windswept landscapes, explore charming villages, and let the salty air and endless horizons fill you with inspiration. You might even write your own Viking saga after a visit to these magical isles.

J is for Jantelov:
 No, it's not a dragon's sneeze, but it might feel like one! Janteloven is the unspoken law of humility, reminding you not to brag about your dragon-slaying skills (even if they're true). Just do your thing, be kind, and let your actions speak louder than your horns.

K is for Kings and Castles:
 Denmark's history is studded with kings, queens, and mighty fortresses. Explore Rosenborg Castle, where royal jewels sparkle like dragons' hoards, or climb Kronborg Castle, the setting of Shakespeare's Hamlet (just don't expect to see any ghosts, unless you have a particularly vivid imagination).

L is for Language Gems:

Learn a few Danish phrases, like "**tak**" (thank you) and "**hej**" (hello), and watch doors (and hearts) open wider than a dragon's treasure cave. Even Vikings appreciated a little effort, and who knows, you might even impress the locals with your charming "**goddag**" (good day).

M is for Museums and Munchies:
From Viking museums packed with ancient artifacts to art galleries showcasing cutting-edge creations, Denmark is a feast for the ...senses and the mind! Dive into Viking history at the National Museum, marvel at modern masterpieces at Louisiana Museum of Modern Art, or satisfy your sweet tooth at the Chocolate Shop in Sønderborg (because chocolate is basically dragon food, right?).

N is for Nature's Wonders:
 Denmark's landscapes are as diverse as a Viking war party. Hike through windswept dunes on Skagen beach, cycle through rolling hills in Jutland, or kayak through serene lakes in the Danish Lake District. Remember, nature is your playground, so explore it with respect and wonder, like a curious bard seeking inspiration for your next epic tale.

O is for Open-mindedness:
Leave your preconceptions at the border and embrace the unexpected. You might find yourself dancing around a bonfire at a Midsummer festival, joining a friendly game of "**kubb**" (a lawn game that might turn Viking-competitive), or learning the secrets of making the perfect "**flæskesteg**" (crispy fried pork belly – trust me, it's epic).

P is for Prices (and pastries!):
 Let's be honest, Denmark isn't the cheapest place to conquer, but the pastries are worth every krone. Budget wisely, pack a few sandwiches for picnics, and remember, experiences are priceless (especially the ones that involve cinnamon rolls the size of your head).

Q is for Quirky Customs:
 Prepare to be surprised! From celebrating Christmas on Christmas Eve to leaving empty chairs for deceased relatives at family gatherings, Denmark has its own set of charming quirks. Embrace them, laugh at them, and add them to your collection of travel-tales to share with friends back home.

R is for Royal Retreats:
 From Fredensborg Castle, a summer haven for Danish royalty, to the majestic Amalienborg Palace in Copenhagen, Denmark is dotted with royal residences. Peek into their grandeur, imagine lavish feasts and dramatic court intrigue, and maybe even fantasize about befriending a prince or princess (just don't expect a dragon as a wedding gift).

S is for Shopping sprees:
From cozy design stores in Copenhagen to charming village markets with handcrafted treasures, Denmark is a shopper's paradise (especially for those who appreciate Viking-inspired beard oil or horned helmets as souvenirs). Just remember, leave room in your suitcase for all the goodies, and maybe avoid buying a live dragon – customs might frown upon that.

T is for Tivoli Gardens:
 This fairytale amusement park in Copenhagen is pure Danish magic. Ride vintage roller coasters, wander through twinkling gardens, and soak up the festive atmosphere. It's like stepping into a storybook, with

less chance of trolls demanding riddles and more chance of delicious ice cream.

U is for Unexpected Encounters:
 Be ready for anything! You might stumble upon a Viking market reenactment, witness a flock of playful seals basking on the rocks, or even strike up a conversation with a local who knows the secret recipe for the best smørrebrød in town. Keep your eyes peeled, your ears open, and your heart ready for the unexpected – that's where the most magical moments lie.

V is for Vikings, obviously!
 From museums packed with artifacts to ancient burial mounds and rune stones, Denmark is a living, breathing testament to the Viking legacy. Learn about their fierce warriors, their cunning traders, and their surprisingly sophisticated culture. You might even discover a hidden Viking within yourself, ready to conquer challenges and forge your own epic saga.

W is for Windmills and Whimsy:

Denmark is powered by wind, both literally and figuratively. Marvel at towering windmills dotting the landscapes, let the playful Danish humor tickle your funny bone, and embrace the whimsical spirit of the people. You might even learn to laugh like a Viking – a loud, hearty below that would make Thor himself proud.

X is for X-perience it all!
 This isn't just a guidebook, it's a call to action. Go beyond the pages, dive into the heart of Denmark, and create your own unique adventure. This is your chance to eat, explore, connect, and make memories that will outlast any index. So grab your metaphorical Viking horns, raise a toast to your Danish odyssey, and remember...

Skål to the journey, the discoveries, and the magic that awaits!

P.S. Don't forget to pack your sense of humor, your willingness to embrace the unknown, and maybe a few extra pastries for the road. You never know when a dragon (or a really good cinnamon roll) might come knocking at your door.

Chapter 20

Acknowledgement

Alright, we've reached the final hurrah, the curtain call, the moment where we raise a toast to all the amazing folks who helped weave this Danish tapestry of adventure! Think of it as our Viking victory shout, echoing across the fjords and forests, praising the heroes who helped us conquer this epic journey.

First and foremost, a deep bow and a hearty "tak" to the people of Denmark themselves. The bakers who fueled our pastries-and-exploration binges, the museum guides who brought history to life with tales of dragons and daring deeds, the locals who smiled and pointed us in the right direction (even when we were hopelessly lost), and everyone who shared their hyggelige havens and infectious laughter – you are the soul of this guide, the warm fire that crackled at the heart of our Danish dream.

A grateful nod to the fellow adventurers too, the bloggers who blazed the trail before us, the photographers whose snaps ignited our wanderlust, and the travel gurus who whispered secrets of hidden gems and quirky festivals. Your stories, your tips, your passion for Denmark – they became our maps and compasses, guiding us through cobbled streets and sun-drenched meadows.

Of course, no epic quest is complete without a trusty crew, so a Viking-sized cheers to me, the writer, my editors, designers, and illustrators who poured their hearts and souls into this guidebook. From crafting words that danced like Northern Lights to conjuring images that made you smell smørrebrød and hear the wind sighing through Viking burial mounds, the joint talent and dedication brought Denmark to life on these pages.

And finally, a wink and a fist bump to you, the intrepid traveler holding this guidebook. You are the reason this whole saga exists, the spark that ignited the Danish flame in our hearts. Your curiosity, your thirst for adventure, your willingness to embrace the unexpected – that's what makes every travel tale worth writing, every map worth unfolding, every fjord worth kayaking through.

So, fellow explorers, raise your tankards of frothy mead, your mugs of steaming coffee, or even just your imaginary dragon-scale goblets (no judgment here!), and let's toast to everyone who made this Danish odyssey possible. Skål to the bakers, the bloggers, the adventurers, the dreamers, and most importantly, to you, the brave soul who dared to conquer Denmark with an open heart and an empty stomach (ready to be filled with pastries, of course).

Because in the end, this guidebook is just a stepping stone, a whisper in the wind, a dragon-shaped compass pointing you towards your own Danish adventure. Let it guide you, inspire you, and most of all, remind you that the greatest treasure isn't found on a map, but in the memories you forge along the way.

So go forth, brave traveler! Explore, wander, laugh, get lost, find yourself, and above all, embrace the hygge. Denmark awaits, with open arms and even warmer ovens. And remember, wherever your journeys take you, carry a piece of Danish magic in your heart, a smidge of Viking spirit in your soul, and the echo of our "**skål**" ringing in your ears.

Until we meet again on some other sun-drenched shore, happy adventures!

P.S. Don't forget to leave a review, share your Danish tale with the world, and maybe even send us a postcard from your hyggeligt hideaway. We'd love to hear how your own Danish odyssey unfolds!

Printed in Great Britain
by Amazon